# A Fragile
# But Marvelous
# Life

# A Fragile But Marvelous Life

## Reader

Aspen Art Museum

for j.a.m.

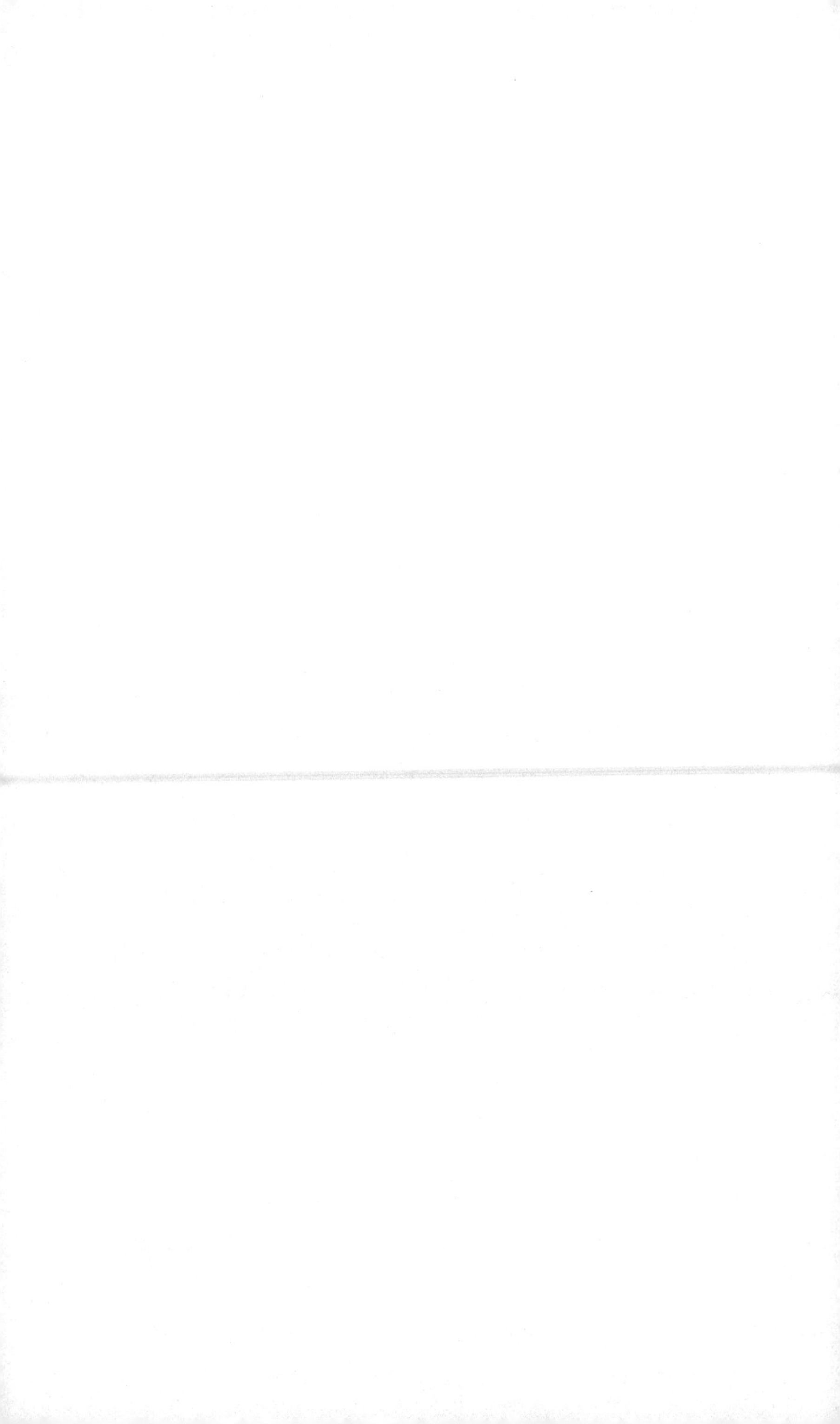

# Introduction

Dear Reader, An Introduction:

As I worked on the exhibition that would become *A Fragile But Marvelous Life*, I read an interview between the artist Robert Breer and filmmaker Jonas Mekas in which Breer explains, "Somewhere, in all my work, I tried to amaze myself with something, and the only way you can amaze yourself is to create a situation in which an accident can happen. The accident is relative to what you're trying to do. It's only an accident because it's unforeseen."[1] It seemed paramount in the making of an exhibition about time, performance, and "liveness" to echo Breer's willingness to embrace chance. As a result, rather than produce a catalogue for the show, we decided to create a companion piece—a compendium or collection of the ideas, research, and conversations that formulated the foundation of the exhibition itself. Consequently, the book took on its own life, exemplifying Allan Kaprow's definition of a Happening: "Something spontaneous, something that just happens to happen."[2]

An excerpt of Kaprow's writing fittingly foregrounds contributions by artists William Pope.L and Emily Roysdon, both of whom address performance's relationship to the political. Pope.L's text "Canary in the Coal Mine," originally printed in *Artjournal* in fall 2011, posits the notion of a "poverty of liveness" within art, asking us to examine what the consequences might be if an absence of real things and bodies continues within the museum. Roysdon has contributed a lecture that she presented at the Museum of Modern Art's 2012 symposium *How Are We Performing Today?* The presentation, which I had the pleasure of attending, was both the seed from which this exhibition grew and the beginning of a larger body of work for Roysdon, one that would continue her examination of the authorization of "alive time" and the management of "liveness." The result would be "Uncounted" (2014), a new text that found its way into the exhibition as a free take-away poster.

An invitation to artist Jason Dodge brought back an incredibly poetic text that illustrates the relation-ship between everyday movement and performance, reminding us that "liveness" occurs simply in the act of being present and paying attention. Following countless conversations and emails with artist Cally Spooner, we decided to include her script, aptly titled "Piece For A Pending Performance," accom-panied by a new introduction addressing the piece's position as "live" and thereby inherently fragile. And finally, it was Spooner who introduced me to Breer's floats—simple, minimal sculptures that glide through space at a speed almost imperceptible to the eye. The opportunity to include an interview with Breer by Charles Levine, one that addresses the cre-ation of the floats in his own words, seemed almost too good to be true.

In another pertinent quote from his interview with Mekas, Breer says of his work: "There was a period when I was searching for something that would be the equivalent of what I thought was—I hate to use these words—mystery…and wonder… killing words…. It's a very fragile thing for me and I felt that it had to be distilled somehow and isolated and it had to be strong; it 'had' to be."[3]

So what you, dear reader, are holding in your hands is a book that like Breer's floats moved at its own speed, open to chance and change. I hope that what you experience in reading it is what we felt in its making—the marvelous experience of being surprised.

## Courtenay Finn, Curator

### Notes

1    Interview with Robert Breer, Jonas Mekas, and P. Adams Sitney on May 13, 1971, *Film Culture*, No. 56–57 (Spring 1973), 42.
2    RoseLee Goldberg, *Performance Art: From Futurism to the Present* (London: Thames & Hudson, 1988), 130.
3    Interview with Robert Breer, Jonas Mekas, and P. Adams Sitney, 41.

# Happenings in the New York Scene 1961

## Allan Kaprow

If you haven't been to the Happenings, let me give you a kaleidoscope sampling of some of their great moments.

Everybody is crowded into a downtown loft, milling about, like at an opening. It's hot. There are lots of big cartons sitting all over the place. One by one, they start to move, sliding and careening drunkenly in every direction, lunging into one another, accompanied by loud breathing sounds over four loudspeakers. Now it's winter and cold and it's dark, and all around little blue lights go on and off at their own speed, while three large brown gunnysack constructions drag an enormous pile of ice and stones over bumps, losing most of it, and blankets keep falling over everything from the ceiling. A hundred iron barrels and gallon wine jugs hanging on ropes swing back and forth, crashing like church bells, spewing glass all over. Suddenly, mushy shapes pop up from the floor and painters slash at curtains dripping with action. A wall of trees tied with colored rags advances on the crowd, scattering everybody, forcing them to leave. There are muslin telephone booths for all with a record player or microphone that tunes you in to everybody else. Coughing, you breathe in noxious fumes, or the smell of hospitals and lemon juice. A nude girl runs after the racing pool of a searchlight, throwing spinach greens into it. Slides and movies, projected over walls and people, depict hamburgers: big ones, huge ones, red ones, skinny ones, flat ones, etc. You come in as a spectator and maybe you discover you're caught in it after all, as you push things around like so much furniture. Words rumble past, whispering, deedaaa, barroom, love me, love me; shadows joggle on screens; power saws and lawn mowers screech just like the I.R.T. at Union Square. Tin cans rattle and you stand up to see or change your seat or answer questions shouted at you by shoeshine boys and old ladies. Long silences when nothing happens, and you're sore because you paid $1.50 contribution, when bang! there you are facing yourself in a mirror jammed at you. Listen. A cough from the alley. You giggle because you're afraid, suffer claustrophobia, talk to someone nonchalantly, but all the time you're *there*, getting into the act . . . Electric fans start, gently wafting breezes of New-Car smell past your nose as leaves bury piles of a whining, burping, foul, pinky mess.

So much for the flavor. Now I would like to describe the nature of Happenings in a different manner, more analytically—their purpose and place in art.

Although widespread opinion has been expressed about these events, usually by those who have never seen them, they are actually little known beyond a small group of interested persons. This small following is aware of several different kinds of Happenings. There are the sophisticated, witty works put on by the theater people; the very sparsely abstract, almost Zen-like rituals given by another group (mostly writers and musicians); and those in which I am most involved—crude, lyrical, and very spontaneous. This kind grew out of the advanced American painting of the last decade, and those of us involved were all painters (or still are). There is some beneficial exchange among the three, however.

In addition, outside New York there is the Gutai group in Osaka; reported activity in San Francisco, Chicago, Cologne, Paris, and Milan; and a history that goes back through Surrealism, Dada, Mime, the circus, carnivals, the traveling saltimbanques, all the way to medieval mystery plays and processions. Of most of this we know very little; only the spirit has been sensed. Of what *I* know, I find that I have decided philosophical reservations. Therefore, the points I make are intended to represent not the views of all those who create works that might be generically related, or even all those whose work I admire, but of those whose works I feel to be the most adventuresome, fruitfully open to applications, and the most challenging of any art in the air at present.

Happenings are events that, put simply, happen. Though the best of them have a decided impact—that is, we feel, "here is something important"—they appear to go nowhere and do not make any particular literary point. In contrast to the arts of the past, they have no structured beginning, middle, or end. Their form is open-ended and fluid; nothing obvious is sought and therefore nothing is won, except the certainty of a number of occurrences to which we are more than normally attentive. They exist for a single performance, or only a few, and are gone forever as new ones take their place.

These events are essentially theater pieces, however unconventional. That they are still largely rejected by devotees of the theater may be due to their uncommon power and primitive energy, and to their derivation from the rites of American Action Painting. But by widening the concept "theater" to include them (like widening the concept "painting" to include collage), we can see them against this basic background and understand them better.

To my way of thinking, Happenings possess some crucial qualities that distinguish them from the usual theatrical works, even the experimental ones of today. First, there is the *context*, the place of conception and enactment. The most intense and essential Happenings have been spawned in old lofts, basements, vacant stores, natural surroundings, and the street, where very small audiences, or groups of visitors, are commingled in some way with the event, flowing in and among its parts. There is thus no separation of audience and play (as there is even in round or pit theaters); the elevated picture-window view of most playhouses is gone, as are the expectations of curtain openings and *tableaux vivants* and curtain closings.

... The sheer rawness of the out-of-doors or the closeness of dingy city quarters in which the radical Happenings flourish is more appropriate, I believe, in temperament and un-artiness, to the materials and directness of these works. The place where anything grows up (a certain kind of art in this case), that is, its "habitat," gives to it not only a space, a set of relationships to the various things around it, and a range of values, but an overall atmosphere as well, which penetrates it and whoever

Allan Kaprow

experiences it. Habitats have always had this effect, but it is especially important now, when our advanced art approaches a fragile but marvelous life, one that maintains itself by a mere thread, melting the surroundings, the artist, the work, and everyone who comes to it into an elusive, changeable configuration.

. . . A Happening is rough and sudden and often feels "dirty." Dirt, we might begin to realize, is also organic and fertile, and everything, including the visitors, can grow a little in such circumstances.

To return to the contrast between Happenings and plays, the second important difference is that a Happening has no plot, no obvious "philosophy," and is materialized in an improvisatory fashion, like jazz, and like much contemporary painting, where we do not know exactly what is going to happen next. The action leads itself any way it wishes, and the artist controls it only to the degree that it keeps on "shaking" right. A modern play rarely has such an impromptu basis, for plays are still *first written*. A Happening is *generated* in action by a headful of ideas or a flimsily jotted-down score of "root" directions.

A play assumes that words are the almost absolute medium. A Happening frequently has words, but they may or may not make literal sense. If they do, their sense is not part of the fabric of "sense" that other nonverbal elements (noise, visual stuff, action) convey. Hence, they have a brief, emergent, and sometimes detached quality. If they do not make sense, then they are heard as the *sound* of words instead of the meaning conveyed by them. Words, however, need not be used at all: a Happening might consist of a swarm of locusts being dropped in and around the performance space. This element of chance with respect to the medium itself is not to be expected from the ordinary theater.

Indeed, the involvement in chance, which is the third and most problematical quality found in Happenings, rarely occurs in the conventional theater. When it does, it is usually a marginal benefit of interpretation. In the present work, chance (in conjunction with improvisation) is a deliberately employed mode of operating that penetrates the whole composition and its character. It is the vehicle of the spontaneous. And it is the clue to understanding how control (the setting up of chance techniques) can effectively produce the opposite quality of the unplanned and apparently uncontrolled. I think it can be demonstrated that much contemporary art, which counts upon inspiration to yield that admittedly desirable verve or sense of the unselfconscious, is by now getting results that appear planned and academic. A loaded brush and a mighty swing always seem to hit the ball to the same spot.

Chance then, rather than spontaneity, is a key term, for it implies risk and fear (thus reestablishing that fine nervousness so pleasant when something is about to occur). It also better names a method that becomes manifestly unmethodical if one considers the pudding more a proof than the recipe.

Traditional art has always tried to make it good

every time, believing that this was a truer truth than life. Artists who directly utilize chance hazard failure, the "failure" of being less artistic and more lifelike. The "Art" they produce might surprisingly turn out to be an affair that has all the inevitability of a well-ordered middle-class Thanksgiving dinner (I have seen a few remarkable Happenings that were "bores" in this sense). But it could be like slipping on a banana peel, or going to heaven.

If a flexible framework with the barest limits is established by selecting, for example, only five elements out of an infinity of possibilities, almost any-thing can happen. And something always does, even things that are unpleasant. Visitors to a Happening are now and then not sure what has taken place when it has ended, even when things have gone "wrong." For when something goes "wrong," something far more "right," more revelatory, has many times emerged. This sort of sudden near-miracle presently seems to be made more likely by chance procedures.

If artists grasp the import of that word *chance* and accept it (no easy achievement in our culture), then its methods needn't invariably cause their work to reduce to either chaos or a bland indifference, lacking in concreteness and intensity, as in a table of random numbers. On the contrary, the identities of those artists who employ such techniques are very clear. It is odd that when artists give up certain hith-erto privileged aspects of the self, so that they cannot always "correct" something according to their taste, the work and the artist frequently come out on top.

And when they come out on the bottom, it is a very concrete bottom!

The final point I should like to make about Happenings as against plays is implicit in all the discussion—their impermanence. Composed so that a premium is placed on the unforeseen, a Happening cannot be reproduced. The few performances given of each work differ considerably from one another; and the work is over before habits begin to set in. The physical materials used to create the environment of Happenings are the most perishable kind: newspapers, junk, rags, old wooden crates knocked together, cardboard cartons cut up, real trees, food, borrowed machines, etc. They cannot last for long in whatever arrangement they are put. A Happening is thus fresh, while it lasts, for better or worse.

Here, we need not go into the considerable history behind such values embodied in the Happenings. Suffice it to say that the passing, the changing, the natural, even the willingness to fail are familiar. They reveal a spirit that is at once passive in its acceptance of what may be and affirmative in its disregard of security. One is also left exposed to the quite marvelous experience of being surprised. This is, in essence, a continuation of the tradition of Realism.

The significance of the Happening is not to be found simply in the fresh creative wind now blowing. Happenings are not just another new style. Instead, like American art of the late 1940s, they are a moral act, a human stand of great urgency, whose professional status as art is less a criterion than their certainty as an ultimate existential commitment.

It has always seemed to me that American creative energy only becomes charged by such a sense of crisis. The real weakness of much vanguard art since 1951 is its complacent assumption that art exists and can be recognized and practiced. I am not so sure whether what we do now is art or something not quite art. If I call it art, it is because I wish to avoid the endless arguments some other name would bring forth. Paradoxically, if it turns out to be art after all, it will be so in spite of (or because of) this larger question.

But this explosive atmosphere has been absent from our arts for ten years, and one by one our major figures have dropped by the wayside, laden with glory. If tense excitement has returned with the Happenings, one can only suspect that the pattern will be repeated. These are our greenest days. Some of us will become famous, and we will have proven once again that the only success occurred when there was a lack of it.

. . . What is not melodramatic, in the sense I am using the word, but is disappointing and tragic, is that today vanguard artists are given their prizes very quickly instead of being left to their adventure. Furthermore, they are led to believe, by no one in particular, that this was the thing they wanted all the while. But in some obscure recess of their mind, they assume they must now die, at least spiritually, to keep the myth intact. Hence, the creative aspect of their art ceases. To all intents and purposes, they are dead and they are famous.

In this context of achievement-and-death, artists who make Happenings are living out the purest melodrama. Their activity embodies the myth of nonsuccess, for Happenings cannot be sold and taken home; they can only be supported. And because of their intimate and fleeting nature, only a few people can experience them. They remain isolated and proud. The creators of such events are adventurers too, because much of what they do is unforeseen. They stack the deck that way.

By some reasonable, but unplanned process, Happenings, we may suspect, have emerged as an art that can function precisely as long as the mechanics of our present rush for cultural maturity continue. This situation will no doubt change eventually and thus will change the issues I address here.

. . . To the extent that a Happening is not a commodity, but a brief event, from the standpoint of any publicity it may receive, it may become a state of mind. Who will have been there at that event? It may become like the sea monsters of the past or the flying saucers of yesterday. I shouldn't really mind, for as the new myth grows on its own, without reference to anything in particular, the artist may achieve a beautiful privacy, famed for something purely imaginary while free to explore something nobody will notice.

Originally published in: Allan Kaprow, *Essays on the Blurring of Art and Life* (Berkeley: University of California Press, 1993), 15–26 (excerpted).

Allan Kaprow

# Interview with Robert Breer 1970

## Charles Levine

An interview with Robert Breer conducted at Breer's home, Palisades, NY, July 1970.

Charles Levine: We are here with Robert Breer in the country. He is sitting on his favorite swivel chair in his studio and it's a beautiful day in July. Bob just told me that the sound of this swivel chair is in a track on one of his films.

Robert Breer: It's in *Breathing*.

CL: How did you record it? You just asked someone else to sit in the swivel...?

RB: No, I recorded it inadvertently.

CL: And then just adapted it?

RB: Well, the track of *Breathing* was the breathing of a neighbor's dog. I got him to make all kinds of weird, low breathing sounds by alternately teasing and baiting him, and pushing away the microphone—which he kept hitting with his tail. During one of those gestures, I made this beautiful, enormous sound with this squeaky chair. I played it back later, and it worked as a piece of punctuation; I found a place for it.

CL: That seems to be like the style you have where you adapt what you find. But at the same time, your work—especially in the last film you've done—is very controlled, very much a thing in which you're adapting one particular line.

I wanted to ask you how you started. In the beginning, you were a painter, right?

RB: Yes. "In the beginning..." sounds kind of biblical; it sounds too pretentious. When I was ten years old, I started being an artist officially in my family, a family of engineers—I drew more than anybody else and I was sent to a Saturday art school. Eventually, that worked into painting by way of army training aids, syphilis posters, and things like that. Those gave me a thorough distaste for any kind of commercial art, and when I got out of the service, I had a big art experience. I could see the possibility of art as being either a boundless pit or an endless horizon. I got very excited about art then. Before, I was just doing it, and I seemed to be able to, but it didn't mean anything. Then, I started painting seriously. But the question was really art in general—I wasn't devoted to painting as such, although I did get very deeply into it.

After I got out of college, I went to Paris on a GI Bill and signed up in a school over there. I never really went to it—no one ever did go to those schools in Paris. People were still painting in the academies that had spiderwebs in them, and they were still painting the nude. It was as if Mondrian hadn't lived in Paris for fifteen or twenty years. The people that I knew were working outside of the schools.

CL: You started working on film during the years you were in Paris. Was it something that you chose as an extension of your painting?

RB: Yes, it was a kind of fluke, really.

CL: Did the mutoscopes enter first, before film?

RB: The first thing that came out of painting was a flip-book, which was a kind of sketch for a movie. It showed the process of painting, rather than any fixed composition. I was interested in examining the process and evolution of the painting over a period of three days—how the forms became locked into each other. The idea of locking them in and then the thing dying on me bothered me, and I was interested in seeing what the process was rather than the end product.

CL: Almost like using the camera to dissect the work?

RB: That's right. In a way, I synthesized films; I have ever since. I started out making the individual frames myself and putting them together. So the first thing was a bunch of moving designs on paper. Then, I filmed those, and the film was entirely different from the one I expected.

CL: Your mutoscopes are sort of like your flip-books. They're a series of cards put into a wheel, which is turned and produces a motion like flipping a book, with lines and drawings together. Did you start them at approximately the same time as you started making films?

RB: No. At first, I made these sketches and I made a film on the basis of those. The idea to make mutoscopes was to bring movies into a gallery situation, where I could have a concrete object that gave this mysterious result of motion. I thought that it would have more impact if you didn't turn out the lights. I wanted it to be in the open, so that you'd really experience this persistence of vision. The idea was also to get people that would go to art galleries interested in looking at this phenomenon instead of the general movie audience just accepting without questioning. All my art ideas had to do with material I was using and I wanted to examine it more closely, and bring it into the open, to expose it. Mutoscopes came along as an afterthought, as a way of presenting flip-books, if you like.

CL: Later, I noticed in your large canvasses that you had motors behind them. You had a small line of metal moving in it, a slow arc that caused a shadow, which was part of the painting in a sense—that seemed like a way of using motion as part of painting.

RB: That's right. I was using the convention of the canvas as a given situation, and then sneaking in elements that normally aren't found in it. And this was, again, a kind of tribute to the art of painting. It's just a matter of crossing over the threshold to get from one convention to another, from cinema back into painting.

CL: I'd like to ask you a question and put you on the spot. What do you think of painting vis-à-vis cinema? You seem to have committed yourself to being a filmmaker rather than a painter.

RB: Well, actually, I have now gone into three-dimensional objects. It's hard to gauge the depth of these involvements, but I've always done everything simultaneously. I mean, since I started making films, I kept on painting for another five or six years. Gradually, I quit painting. But then I started going into these objects.

CL: All of your work seems to incorporate some sort of movement. There are pieces that move across the floor, paintings that have motors behind them, mutoscopes turning, and films, of course, that move through projectors. I wonder whether you felt that movies were better than painting?

RB: Even in a painting, the clue to what I do has something to do with ambiguity and controlling ambiguity and making it dramatic. Shapes and relationships are very complex and are played off each other. The ambiguity was there as a very definite element, even in a static painting. With film, I broke up the continuity of the flow in such a way that sometimes it's hard to tell whether the film is going forwards or backwards. This is another way of using material to get ambiguity as an expressive feature of the thing.

CL: Have you felt that there is any relationship to your work and musical structures?

RB: I suppose only to the extent that one is aware of structure. There is no conscious relation at all. As a matter of fact, it's one of the things I want to get away from, because this was what happened in many early films—Micky-Mousing image to sound. The weakness of many abstract films is the idea of composing imagery to a track, and this is done all the time, of course, in commercial cinema. For me, it was something to escape, to avoid. I always work in silence. What I wanted to emphasize was the visual structure, and sound has a way of taking over, so I always put my sound in afterwards. If there's a connection, it certainly is not deliberate.

My first films were silent, and in later films, I have long silent passages, helpful silences where the image has to take over—it makes everybody look back at the projection booth to see if somebody up there died.

CL: I'd like to ask you about the things that move across the floor. At Rauschenberg's, when I first saw them, they were like little flat platforms. They would come to one wall, they had motors in reverse, and then they would keep going in the other direction. I don't know how they have progressed, but you got to the point where they are included at the Japanese World Fair.

RB: The ones in Osaka are six feet high and six feet in diameter. You saw the souvenirs that were made from those big pieces. In Japan, they are at the pavilion for the Pepsi-Cola Company, or as we refer to it now, the "well-known soft drink company." Everything around the pavilion, inside and outside, was designed by a group of artists, including myself, working through an organization called Experiments in Art and Technology (E.A.T.). It took us two years.

The things outside are my major contribution— these things I call "floats" (other people call them "creepies"), these large dome-shaped objects that are motorized underneath by batteries. We were talking about film, and the way I got into these floats is obviously through motion. Ironically enough, these things move, but the speed is so slow it's barely perceptible. When you're standing there, one might bump into you, but you don't really notice it. Of course, with the films, they're so fast you also almost don't realize that they're moving either.

In looking back at what I've done, I've played with thresholds of perception very closely. In the case of the concrete object, it is something so improbable that it would move, but lo and behold, it does. With cinema, it's the other way around.

CL: I heard you say something like the Japanese felt they were too slow. Do they move at a similar speed to the ones I saw?

RB: Yeah, they are very slow. The irony, of course, is that the reason I got involved with the Japanese project at all was because of a reference made about my objects being similar to the rocks in the temple gardens of Japan. These rocks were apparently supposed to move if you sat there long enough and contemplated them. This was kind of a poetic equivalent to what I was doing and when the opportunity came to do something in Japan, I got interested in that kind of transcultural situation.

CL: The actual speed doesn't have that much to do with how you perceive the object, though. I suppose if they were moving at fifty miles an hour, it would be rather frightening...

RB: This was suggested to me by the directors of the well-known soft drink company—to speed them up. It was difficult for me to explain to them that the idea was more of creating a presence, rather than some kind of spectacle, some kind of jazzy situation. The whole essence of these things is in the inscrutability of their motion, the fact that you can't predict where they're going. As soon as they're sped up fast enough to tell where they're going, then it becomes a predictable situation and instant monotony.

CL: It sort of reminds me of those old electric cars that used to be out in Coney Island where you'd drive around in circles. It would take away the whole mysterious quality of the object that moves, but doesn't have a particular utilitarian view in mind—the very shape of them is not utilitarian.

RB: Yes. The floats are basically inanimate objects.

They are rather dumb-looking in that sense. They have amorphous shapes, somewhat geometrical, but not too specific. They do look static when you look at them. When you realize that they are moving around, and of course there are several of them moving in relation to each other, then motion itself is something that is outside of them, not a part of them. You don't have a piece with something moving on it, the piece itself is moving, and what I hope happens is that their movement is an essence like the air around them. In this way, I've isolated motion itself. That's what I was trying to do with film too, going back and forth over a flow—the flow of motion—stopping at a time so that you could sense it when it did get into action.

CL: It's almost like a sort of free-form mechanical painting dance. Like two of these things could come together and the engines would reverse and then they would separate.

RB: That's right. They recompose themselves on this flat terrace, in this case, in Japan. And everywhere that these run around, they have autonomy, they get into situations, they create anecdotes by bumping into things. But as far as formal composition is concerned, it's random. And this pleases me very much—I started something and then it goes on its way, it's kind of a Pygmalion situation.

Originally published in: *Film Culture*, No. 56–57 (1973), 55–68 (excerpted).

# Canary in the
# Coal Mine 2011

## William Pope.L

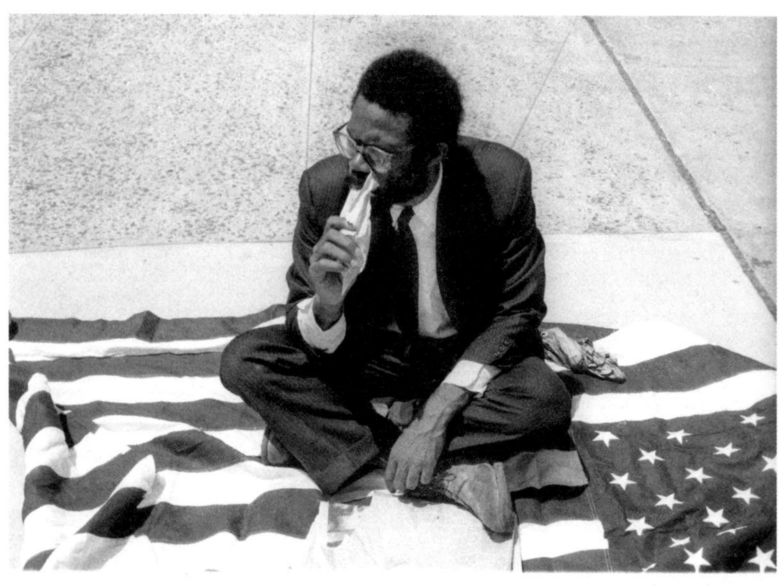

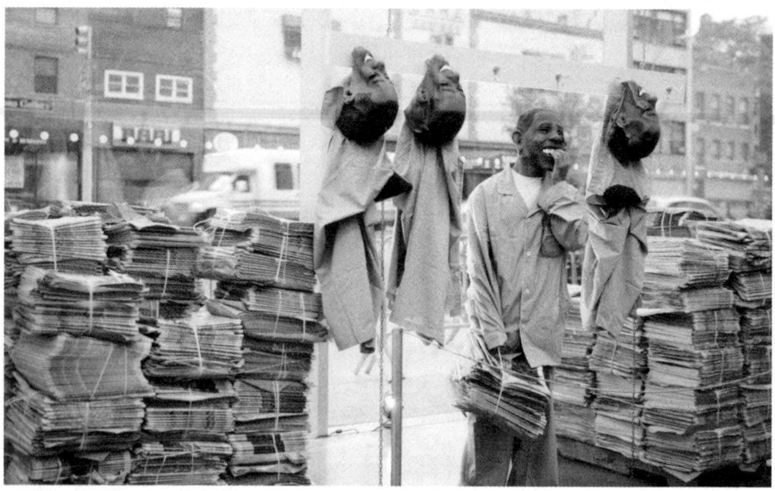

William Pope.L, *Eating the Wall Street Journal (New Millenium version)*, 2010. Courtesy the artist and Mitchell-Innes & Nash, New York. © Pope.L. Photo: Benoit Pailey

William Pope.L, *Eating the Wall Street Journal (early street version)*, 1991. Courtesy the artist and Mitchell-Innes & Nash, New York. © Pope.L. Photo: James Pruznick

0.  Institutionalized art performance reenactment is about emptying as much as it is
about remembering. Memory is a smoke
screen for a set of anxieties possessed by
both the packrat and the king. Both hoard
to defend some unspoken, unrecognized
absence. Both use the myopia of repetition to pleasure their perspective and
bestow upon their project an illusion of
progress and community.

.01  Warhol's object production was an
incredibly narrow, near-perfect bit of institutionalized art performance. If everything
is an object then no one gets near, no one
gets in, no one gets hurt. His performance
created pleasure by reproducing a poor
representation of a thing. The thing itself
incited pleasure, a sense of safety in
the familiar. The poverty of the objects
signaled something lost. A poverty of liveness? Maybe the absence of real things and
bodies helps us to keep afloat the fantasy
that we are above being alive.

1.  Karaoke is an example of performance
reenactment in which participants derive

pleasure by knowingly reperforming that which has been reperformed many times before. A poorly performed example can be a terrific example. Drinking alcohol, loud carousing, singing off-key late into the darkness collaborate in a ritual obliteration, the goal being: community-cohesion via public obliteration. Can you reenact something until it's rendered completely invisible? Until its true color finally shows through? A transparent color suffused in dust, cobwebs, and melancholy?

1.1 Performance reenactment has been an important part of Fluxus art practice for some time now and serves a similar function as it does for karaoke: group cohesion. The ritual repetition of some action or event by a group helps to mark that group off from another. The reenactment as reenacted is the ultimate thing. The concerns and fears of the group are contained in the repetition. The difference between reenactments is negligible. Reenacting empowers the group and disempowers originality, craft, the author, and property.

1.01 However, there is a strong element of self-consciousness in Fluxus; for example, the obsession with documentation. If karaoke is memorialized via the hangover, Fluxus is memorialized via the boxed performance relic. Notwithstanding Fluxus's utopic desire to level the playing field of art, the issue of quality still matters. Unlike karaoke, differences between performers and performances in Fluxus are tracked very carefully.

1.2 Fluxus is part of the avant-garde tradition, and its early rationales were platformed on challenges to property, the author, and originality. Today, these rationales remain, but rub uncomfortably against the movement's more businesslike attitudes. So—when Fluxus is happening and the status quo isn't burning, what is being obliterated?

2. The recent attempts to institutionalize performance art by major museums and galleries mark a desire to make packaged objects of a form. Performance art as a form is unique because of its live character,

its supposed unrepeatability, which has allowed it to slip and slide through the cracks of the market. Indeed, cultural institutionalization usually involves strategies that maximize profit, use, or value by enabling the multiple consumption of a product. The ideal is to sell a single product as many times as possible. Unlike karaoke or Broadway, art performance typically secures its rep via very few performances; sometimes, we only know of certain canonical performances via legend.

2.2 The collecting of performance objects, residues, props, scores, and zines laid the groundwork for the end of the idea of live performance as the final defense against the "sale." The advent of videotape was the penultimate nail in the coffin. Suddenly, the vaunted unrepeatability of performance was in question. Even so, a videotape is not the thing itself. However, if an idea or a piece of music or a novel or a sports star can be sold, why not a performance? What is a performance, but a bundle of ideas? Theater has been selling bundles of ideas for a few centuries.

2.3 Is resistance to the art market essential for performance art? Did its celebrated slippery resistance ever truly exist?
Is resistance an obsolete concept for today's consumers?

3. For my money, resistance to established power is always necessary, even if, especially if, the established power is radical, avant-garde, or subversive.

3.1 Or a gleaming castle on a hill that sells artworks, snacks, and central heating.

4. Yes, let's set aside reenactment, performance art, liveness, and institutionalization for a moment and focus on bigger fish, like social responsibility.

4.1 Let's put our foot down and state something significant: resistance itself is a product. What would real resistance look like? Real resistance always looks like betrayal 'cause it's extremely difficult, if not impossible, to defeat an enemy and not become the enemy.

4.01 Let's say live performance art is some kind of canary in the coal mine. What is its death trying to tell us? Or more interestingly, its middle years, what are they trying to tell us about a form that lives and dies on liveness? And what does it mean for art making not only as a practice, but also as a business?

5. After life, we, performance artists, should sell what? Tacos? Medical supplies for diabetes? Real estate in California? No, the real shit, the next shit, is the soul. I don't know if it actually exists, but I know almost everybody wants one.

5.1 And in terms of marketing, if it doesn't exist, that makes it even more special.

5.01 So—the next product for us, performance artists, to sell is the soul. Not our own, of course. Why would we want to do that? But the thing itself.

5.2 And let's say for argument's sake, we've already established our practice. Business is good. We've amputated a foot or a hand or a leg or a sex part here or there, always thinking at the back of our minds that if things get really tough we've still got the organs and the head. Then, of course, the hard times arrive, maybe they stay too long, until one day, the only thing we have left to sell is whatever is essential that makes us human—

Originally published in: *artjournal*, Vol. 70, No. 3 (Fall 2011), 55–58. Courtesy the artist and Mitchell-Innes & Nash, New York.

William Pope.L

# Notes on Performance and Institutions, Notes on Transitions, To Discompose 2012

## Emily Roysdon

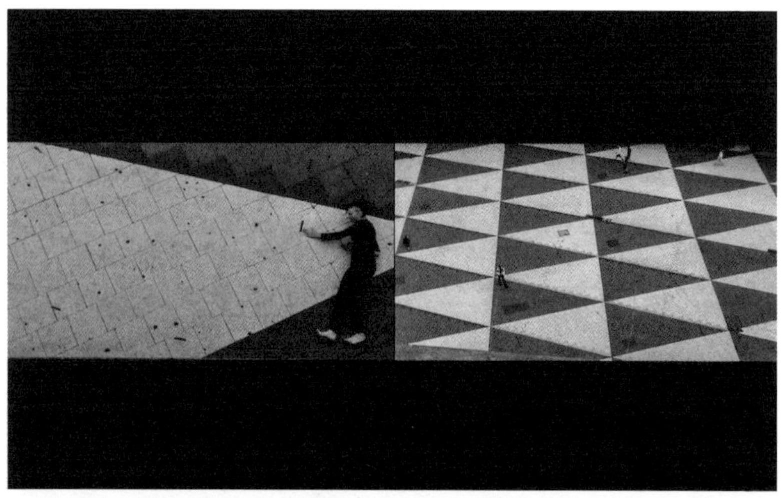

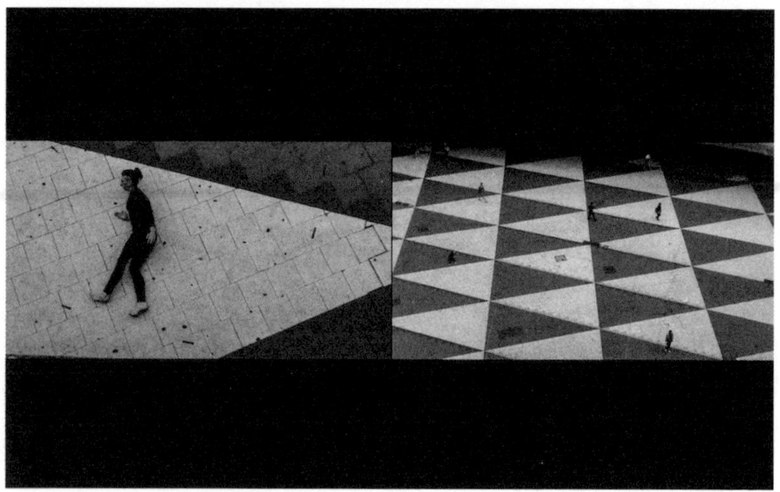

Emily Roysdon, *Sense and Sense*, 2010 (stills). Two-channel video (color, silent); 15:25 min. Courtesy the artist

Today, I am using the projection behind me to represent two things. Firstly, it's a performance video I made in 2010 titled *Sense and Sense*. The project was made in Stockholm and takes aim at the city's central public square, Sergels torg. Designed as part of the social democratic state to be the site of political manifestations in the city, the square is, in fact, used as such. I was interested in use and proper use. In regulation and improvisation. If one site is designed for political speech, what happens to the rest of the city?

Importantly, the abstract pattern of the square is also the graphic identity and representation of the city on posters, announcements, etc. This repeating pattern symbolizes Stockholm—an abstraction representing free movement, representing a city or an idea of a city. I wanted to use the vernacular movement of the place—walking—to explore the complex and abstract ideas of the site, so I asked MPA, my collaborator, friend, and interlocutor for ten years, to walk on her side.

We didn't practice, but we talked about how to create the illusion of movement. You have to push your shoulder harder into the ground and lift your hip in order to move your leg forward. The arm precedes the leg. Keep the feet flexed. Keep the butt tucked in—if the butt starts to triangulate in the back you lose the sense of verticality.

This project has two channels. You are only seeing one—the wide shot, the shot with context, and thus, the more political image. The other channel is a more intimate portrait of the physical struggle needed to create this illusion of movement. The two channels together, near and far, solo and contextualized images, are the illusion and struggle of movement.

So the first thing it is, is all of this. Making a point regarding what a place is built for and how it is used.

And the second thing it is, today, is a clock. This performance took fifteen minutes, from one side of the public square to the other, so I will use this to tell time: real time, outside time, public time, body time, abstract time. My fifteen minutes transposed to that fifteen minutes. And by the time MPA has crossed

Sergels torg, I will have told you a little bit about myself, introduced two projects, and thrown in a few more things…

I didn't begin my education as an artist. Instead, I studied international politics. I had a mentor, Eqbal Ahmad, who died while I was his student. I was in the office of another faculty member, Margaret Cerullo, when it happened. On a previous day, she had said, "We're here, we're queer, and we're not going shopping." That made a big impression. But when Eqbal died, I let go a little and slipped into a photography class. The first things that I really remember turning me on were David Wojnarowicz and pictures of Judson Church dances. Those bodies, and arrangements, sweatpants and running, chairs, mattresses, flags, and falling, all arrested in black and white.

For the ten years since, I've been thinking about the primacy of movement—how people move socially, politically, formally, publicly, aesthetically, and experimentally. I began by focusing on the relationship between image and movement, then moving into

an expanded field of choreography—one
not bound to dance, but equally relevant
to collectivities and organizing. I've used
photography, printmaking, and curating as
strategies. I've made performances in streets,
squares, and black boxes. I've written lyrics
for bands—texts with life that get repeated
nightly. And recently, I've made costumes
for choreographers. After years of showing
up to watch, I wanted to participate on
their terms, within their structures and
institutions, through collaborative roles. I've
been an artist, an audience member, and a
collaborator in a variety of institutions. To
be at early-phase building rehearsals, to be
backstage, to be in dialogue.

Ten years, fifteen minutes, naming time. Eras,
elections, rehearsal. Is "rehearsal" a name
for a kind of time or a need of a group? Are
either of these things able to be supported in
a museum—this kind of time or need?

For the past year, I've been interested in
transitions. Choreographic, interpersonal,
governmental, the shifting of weight, changing of direction. Transitions, no matter the

context, are a political moment. The choreographic detaches itself from any position of certainty. It is full of transitions. I came to thinking about transitions through another vocabulary set that had guided me in previous years—the relationship between struggle and improvisation. I'm very much interested in a performative vocabulary that can articulate movement and the politics of struggle and improvisation. Transitions, no matter the context. A shift, a choice, a question, a policy. Is this museum, any museum, in transition?

With every passing, any awareness of time, the choreographic discomposes the space around us, asking how we arrange our bodies in response.

What can we take as a score for this transition, for this response? One thing we know well is "le bench." The bench that goes with some paintings. It's a score, even a script. As Robin Bernstein says in her text "Dances with Things: Material Culture and the Performance of Race," "The term 'script' denotes not a rigid dictation of performed action but, rather, a necessary openness to resistance, interpretation, and improvisation."[1] I'm looking for a script, a score for this transition—a conversation, an underground magazine, that bench—material and immaterial things that can prompt, inspire, or structure this thinking. Looking at some things and people already in the museum, consider Lucinda Childs's masterpiece *DANCE*, a collaboration with Philip Glass and Sol LeWitt from 1979. About this work, Childs has explained that the conflict between the image and the dancer was very much intended. I know that she is referring to LeWitt's projection onto the dancers and I know this is formal and that *DANCE* is the title of the work, but what if we extended the metaphor into all elements of this collaboration: Glass's monumental repetition with variation; LeWitt's perspective and scale-altering projection; Childs's rigorous, epic, continuous movement. Some of these elements, adjectives, are of the house already built. For is not traditional exhibition making monumental repetition with variation? And then some of the elements are strategies for how to recognize conflict in that house—rigorous, continuous, scale-altering, movement…

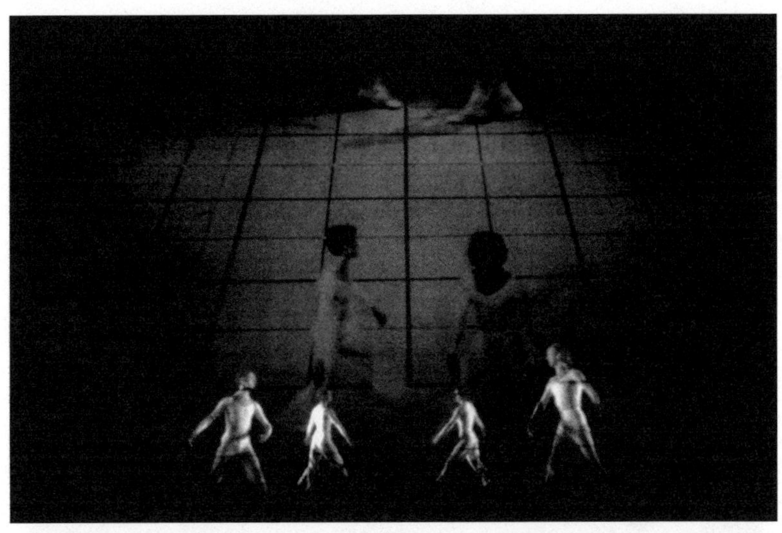

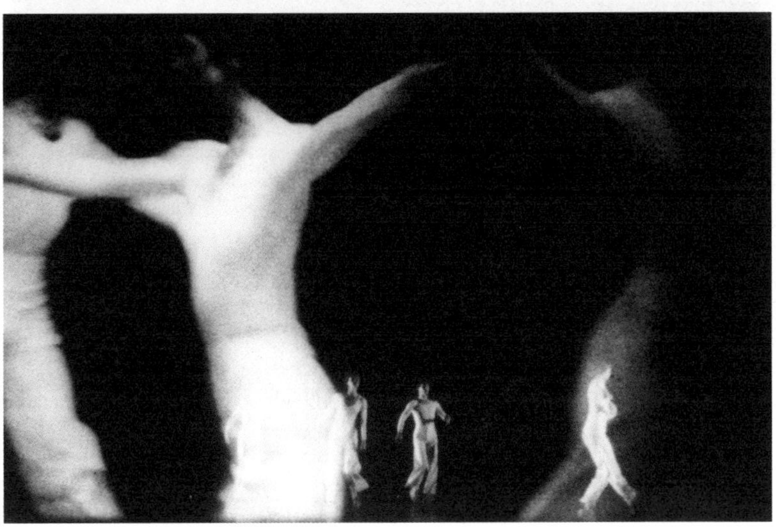

Lucinda Childs, *DANCE*, 1979. Courtesy the artist. Photo: © Nathaniel Tileston

Emily Roysdon

Could this collaboration and conflict, movement and image, be a score for the performance department, for the disciplinary boundaries of the art institution?

What else can be a score? There is so much already inside the museum that can be looked to. And, of course, a museum is always thinking about its public—the one imagined and created simultaneously. The one to whom much of this desire for performance in the museum is attributed.

Gertrude Stein has said: "The only thing that is different from one time to another is what is seen and what is seen depends upon how everybody is doing everything."[2] What is seen. How everybody is doing everything.

In 1926, Stein wrote "Composition as Explanation" to talk about time-sense, distribution, using everything, and a continuous present. She wasn't talking about photography or choreography, but she could have been. In her elliptical, if narrow, statement on epochal thinking, imaging and representation ("what is seen," difference) are aligned with the ability, potential, and mechanics of the body and technology ("how everybody is doing everything"). To which I add: How everybody is doing everything is what is different, and how difference is seen. What is seen depends upon how everybody is doing.

How everybody is doing everything. Stein's "everybody" opens the door to the public. And her grand formulation, "everybody… everything," is the precise counterpoint to the questions of use, regulation, movement, scripting, performance, collectivity, collections, and disciplinarity that we're thinking about here. I am using Stein's sentence to enter an arena of publics—counter-publics, queer publics, and sub-publics—adding to my consideration of movement as discomposition. How we use space constitutes the nature of our political selves. Stein is writing about composition, but in the process, she is discomposing language. I am talking about performance and publics, and how in process, they discompose the museum. To discompose space, instead of renewal, instead of transgression, or even decomposition. To discompose is to let the structure reveal itself as you walk by. It is to take the whole operations of the museum in, not just what is inside the frame.

Now, I can quickly introduce two projects relevant to these questions and vocabularies before MPA has traversed this square.

In 2010, I was invited by Matthew Lyons to make a project at the Kitchen. *A Gay Bar Called Everywhere (With Costumes and No Practice)*, a collaborative performance project, began with the idea that all of Susan Sontag's life and work took place in a gay bar. She never left the table. People come and go—styles, decades, regimes, and theories. This scene led the way to a loose formulation about performance, performativity, and theorizing the struggle and ingenuity of queer life. The scene of the gay bar, *Everywhere*, the refuge, ethics, desire, violence, telling, rubbed up alongside the history of feminist intellectuals and the history of the Kitchen. I invited participating artists to respond to this formulation. The "no practice" thing was true. We were all on stage together the whole time, watching each other's formulations unfold and being directed, live, as to how we could participate in each artist's piece. Collaborators included: Barbara Hammer, Nicole Eisenman, JD Samson, A.L. Steiner, K8 Hardy, MPA, Yve Laris Cohen, Will Rawls, Nao Bustamante, Vanessa Anspaugh, Thomas Lax, Jibz Cameron, to name a few.

In spring 2012, I was commissioned by Catherine Wood and Kathy Noble at Tate Modern to make a project for their series Tate Live Performance Room that is broadcast, live, online. *I am a Helicopter, Camera, Queen* was my response to their quite specific invitation. Given that it was a series, each artist would use the same room and have the same one-camera technical setup. I asked for volunteers who were willing to identify as queer and/or feminist to perform the room with me, to make room, reconstruct an already heavily signified space, and to create a stage within their collectivity. One hundred and five people participated in the choreography.

I was thinking of the helicopter, camera, and queen as representations of territory and seeing, regimes of viewing and ways of understanding space. I had a very formal reaction to the room itself and then my thoughts became dominated by the camera, which takes the place of the live audience. And to this, I wanted to have a more hysterical reaction. I wanted the room to be full when the live stream opened, for a lot of people to look back on the one person "on their own device" at home. So I developed the work in two parts with a transition in between—formal and hysterical. And here, I use the word "discompose" again: to build and then discompose the space. We pushed against the walls and then we exceeded them—moving into and regrouping in the Turbine Hall, a famously enormous space, to take another form on another scale.

There was a room-size vinyl score on the floor. The walls buttressed by language on the perimeter. There were three slight strings pulled across the room just above head height as another (minimal) way of marking scale and dividing space. They later get taken down and snipped to pieces and attached to the camera lens—to dress up the camera once we'd allowed it into the room. I used newspapers as title cards that punctuated the performance—with slips of signage that read: "Life from the Tote Madern." Newspaper as an analog technology mixed in with other questions of distribution—legibility that Kathy and Catherine had framed in their invitation.

At the risk of over-simplifying this work, or my practice, but in service of the particularity of this event: part of my pleasure as an artist is asking questions and figuring out how to do things with people—framing, composing, thinking with, and through my peers' practices. My vocabulary here—of movement, struggle, improvisation, transitions, to discompose—is from where I make work, and how I try to create collaborative structures for people to be alive inside.

I wanted to finish with a few questions:
Can the language of the choreographic be exploited to create space?
Collectivities instead of collections. Is this a question? Can we support collectivities instead of collections?
What can we take as a score?
How and when will art institutions learn from performance ones?
Is rehearsal a name for a kind of time or a need of a group?

Emily Roysdon

How can museums avoid acting like the police in regards to performance?

R. E. S. P. E. C. T. the lives you invite in here.

Is this a question: how to be alive in a museum? (By the way, I Googled this question just to see what would come up: spiders, Elvis, and a fundraising event with floral arrangements that interpret masterworks. So yes, I think it's a good question to ask—we need better answers.)

How to be alive in a museum: have needs, rehearse, listen, work the room, ask for help, take rest, use everything, look back, look around, use everything, walk, dance, discompose, ask for help.

Notes

1    Robin Bernstein, "Dances with Things: Material Culture and the
     Perfomance of Race," *Social Text* 27 (2009), 68.
2    Gertrude Stein, "Composition as Explanation," Lecture: Cambridge and
     Oxford University, June 4 and 7, 1926.

Originally presented at: The Annual Performance Symposium at MoMA: How
Are We Performing Today? New Formats, Places, and Practices of Performance-
Related Art, Saturday, November 17, 2012, 1–7 PM.

# Piece For A Pending Performance <sub>2011</sub>

## Cally Spooner

Hello! I'm Tom.

Today, I've come to show you how I changed
my life, by turning myself into a cooperator,
and an operator of communication, in public.
Today, I'll show how you too can turn your
lives around and escape your stunted private
existence, and hatch into a contemporary
worker, like me.
Today, I'll be demonstrating the benefits of
acting, active, *together*.
Using our minds, working our words,
increasing our speed, maxing our mobility,
I ask you to join me, today, to make new
temporary friends and influence people.
Here.
Now.
Together.
Out.
Not in.
Welcome.
*This* is a good, good place to be.
This, I can assure you.
Now, since I began to work in this field, I'm
stronger, faster, and much better looking. I
have, quite literally, evolved. I'm thinking
fast, speaking fast, on my feet, always moving,

very fast, sometimes by foot, mostly by bus,
day in, day out, out and about, always out, in
the company of others.
Listen, listen.
To me.
To you.
Let's chat.
It's good, good times.
I'm on top of the world.
Now...
What you see here is what you get, and what
you get is good.
Right here, right now, I am who I am, and
who I am is public.
Suited, booted, fabulously controlled.
That's me.
I'm feeling good, join in, and you can feel
good too.
Join me and WATCH as private life *dissolves*
along with all those irritating local niggles;
petty private concerns... and I can tell you
now it has been VERY nice since those little
domestic commitments left.
Silly private struggles...
Thankless tasks...
Others.
That's right, ladies and gents, I can assure

you that I have NEVER received a round of
applause at home.
So!
As you might have noticed, I'm a public kind
of guy.
I've given up on home.
It's not for me.
I'm in the business of communication, and
home is not the place for that.
And, so, I *urge* you, PLEASE look beyond
your fixed routines.
*This* is freedom.
THIS is an adventure.
A rebellion of the heart!
The triumph of work over will, in the
presence of others.
Today, we will turn ourselves into performers
of pure live activity; we'll bask in the
limelight, using *only* our minds, our mouths,
and some very, very good manners.
We WILL be the most talkative members of
working polite society, 24/7, with a 100%
money-back guarantee that every move we
make, every step we take, someone will
be listening, and THIS will DOUBLE our
excellence.
Tom! I hear you cry.

How can I do that?
How can I start to work like you?
Well, I'll tell you exactly what I tell them all:
Conversation.
That's right, folks, it's time to take a deep
breath and join an ever increasingly
intellectualized living labor force.
Tom! I don't understand!
Well, frankly, neither do I, but I CAN assure
you that the thrill of a crowd, the flexibility of
conditional friendships, and the attentiveness
of faces you can't quite see, will affirm that
yes, YES. You have truly arrived.
Now…
The conditions for this kind of public work
are very specific, and they do need to be
shared. The workspace does need to be used
by very many people, and while from time
to time I have, of course, been working from
what we could call "home" (which I have
since decommissioned, as such), and I did
have something a little more… official…
I gave it up.
Didn't like it.
Didn't need it……
Quite liked it, in a way……
Had a lovely little cactus, just there, Radio 3

playing, visitors popping by, sharing thoughts, feelings, about production, without product, and so forth.

BUT.

Given the nature of my very public work it became… let's say—inappropriate—to conduct any professional liaisons in the privacy of a four-walled room, with a nice high ceiling… beautiful third-story window… sturdy closable door… low rent … cups of… tea.

So, I hit the road!

Because a desk is ONLY good for admin.

Now…

Because the right conditions for this kind of work are *essential*, I have noticed that, perhaps, several of you are not quite engaged to the extent that we could fully say you were particularly cooperating. And in this case, cooperation is *essential*. So, if I could just ask you all to look at me now, and not look anywhere but here, and then perhaps if I go first and start to speak, and then you can speak after that, and so forth, and this way we'll be achieving a productively nonproductive interaction with people we don't really know, which is what we call in

this business "a dialogue."
Lovely.
Good.
So.
I do need to just grab your attention, and for me, that's never been a problem.
I've been told I'm very enigmatic. Charming even. *"Ahhhh. Tom."*
They say.
*"He's a charmer."*
And that's a good, strong tool to work with.
So!
I've been putting it to work.
Throwing it out, bringing it back, and what came back?
Offers.
The heart is here, and here we all are, in public, and all I need to do is keep myself clean, never get tired, never grow old, stay light, stay easy, it's easy, ahead of the game, to keep on learning, learning to earn a fairly irregular tax-free salary, which occasionally covers costs.
Working through thinking, thinking through working, working as thinking, as we all become purely, invisibly PRODUCTIVE.....
But now...

Sorry...

I am just ever so slightly concerned that, perhaps, you are just a little bit near my space... right here... so... now, I'll just establish this space here, which is where I will be working from today...

Good.

Good.

Yes.

See, this is my space. Today. Good.

So!

Tom! What will I need? What will I do? What am I doing? Where will I work from? What is all this? Am I ok? Well, ladies and gentlemen, these are all *very* fair questions, and I can tell you now, with complete enthusiasm: You will work EVERYWHERE.

Tom! I hear you ask. What will I need?

You will need a suit.

Tom! What are your tools?

Your mind and your soul.

Tom! That sounds a bit weird, and not in a good way.

Yes it does!

Tom, what will I do?

You will communicate unstoppably.

Tom! What will I communicate?

You will communicate communication.
Tom! I'm confused.
That's ok!
Will I work quickly? Yes you will.
Will I work nosily? Yes you will!
Will I work alone. NO you will NOT!
Will I need a desk? Possibly for admin.
Tom! What will I *produce*? Well, ladies and gents. You will produce *nothing*.
You will do this in front of others.
And they will clap.
So.
There you have it.
I'm a man of many words and limited material.
I just need what I need, and I certainly don't think it's a working standard to have anything other than a good suit, a bus with no changes, and an economically viable briefcase, which will do.
Here.
And it's not cheap.
Just standard.
And although from time to time one may require a stable…
Moment.
Just stay strong!

Think of all the offers you'll bump into simply by keeping light on your feet!
But Tom! I'm simply not flexible.
Tom! How *are* you doing this?
How *is* he doing this?
Granted.
It's amazing.
But once was exactly where you are now.
I spent *years* on the wrong side of another man's performance.
Standing in line, working my turn.
A cog!
But since I've turned my insides outside, I can adapt to the most sudden convergences. I can SWITCH from one set of rules to another, from day to day, place to place, people to people, small and light. I'm every man, I'm every woman. Light and flexible. I have no surplus, I leave no trace. Just me and my mind. Just you and your thoughts. Light on my feet, so we can begin to... Errrrrr ......
to seek... the very best. The better than best. It's just right ...... here ...... inside
...... After all...... only nothing comes from nothing, and as I am certainly saying something, here is...
My stage.

Your space.
My mind.
Your presence.
Lovely.
So.
Today, we will learn it is not what we make
from what we do, but simply that we "do,"
together; Opportunism, social integration,
inexhaustible and cheerful resignation!
Ladies and gents, that's us! And I'm HAPPY
that we can achieve....
Not results...
Just...
Activity...
Not productive?
No!
I have transcended results!
I embraced CHOICE! ...
I *choose* whether I'm speaking too much,
whether I've been out enough, whether I've
been in enough, maybe too much, maybe
too little, maybe... whether you're listening,
maybe you're laughing... at me... perhaps...
But as a man of the *highest* intellectual labor
patterns, I relish this!
I DO!
Just so long as you're all listening....

It's me and you and you and me you see?
We're together? See? We'll need to talk.
Have a chat. Have a dinner. Would you like
dinner? Can I have dinner? Will you call
back? Of course… they'll call back. Left a
message. Very clear. Forty seconds. Maybe
more… think it went fine. It's fine, because…
I'm choosing my own success… and what
is success? Tom! What is success? You're
saying. Aren't you just thinking; Tom! What
is success? To which I will reply.
Not results.
Not exactly.
Not quite sure…
Exactly what…
But excellence is almost guaranteed and…
… certainly just within grasp.
And we will achieve it as soon as I find
my……
Dialogue.
Hmmmm.
I think…
You see…… usually in this situation, I would
have someone, to interrupt me.
Usually, at this point, I think someone
might… join in. It's more like a play that
way. You know… I say something, they say

something else, I speak back, have a word, and so forth. It works well. It's a nice little device, nice little number I've been using for years now. But… well… there's no one to … I just need a soundboard you see.

An other.

To work with.

Because I'm a subject of communication, so to speak. To speak. I will speak. That's my motto: subjects of communication.

SUBJECTS OF COMMUNICATION.

Because *I* am not a monologue.

I can't achieve with a monologue…

… a fucking monologue.

I AM NOT A MONOLOGUE!!!

Here now, just here, got to, find some. Offers. Some people. Some…

Prospects……

…Are EVERYWHERE.

The exchanges are everywhere.

Please, will you please begin your exchanges, your interactions with me, please, please just give me something to work with here. I have nothing. Everywhere. It's just not mutually cooperative to not cooperate. And why does this keep arising?

WHY?

It is so irrelevant; it is stupid and irrelevant
to the work. I don't want a monologue. It
would NOT be helpful, it would not be
helpful. It is superfluous. It would impede
me, it is decorative.
No one has monologues.
No one. Has. Monologues. These. Days. And I
am VERY these days……
because the point is… Words!
Words!
And… Dialogue you see….
… loaded with…
Interactions with…
…people.
People! Listen, listen here now, know we
can ALL be active together! Idle hands,
ladies and gents, idle hands! But ALL
making of things is idle in these new and
improved times of making without making.
Action not form! And the activity is…
nothing… well it's… nothing… But the
purest… communication.
Everything out!
Everything seen!
Everything heard!
Words heard! Persuasion seen!
Out! Out! Out! Out!

Work! Work! Now, now please produce …
the activity.
And I am HAPPY.
Because, I know you are expecting, and I am
ready, I am already, working! I am ALWAYS
working… I am here, I am present, prepped,
ready, I am VERY now. I am here, I am
now. I'm ready. I'm present, I am absolutely
fucking present. I am LIVE.
I am so contemporary I am only here. I am
only *present*. I am here to present…
Present. Here, now, nothing. Nothing.
In my right hand.
Nothing.
In my left hand.
Nothing.
Under my hat? I'm not wearing a hat!
LISTEN! LISTEN! Now! Respond! I am. SO
busy. I am SO busy. I am SPEAKING! I am
delivering, I have something to say and I
will say it!
And I can see that maybe I'll just leave by
the door… and hope that maybe… you
might join me in this … incredibly important
moment in the development of a new and
dynamic practice of producing.
Dialogue.

Because today, we are in a golden age; the development of activity, without work! Which is how I have KICKED the habit of monologues, and achieved excellence, in public, with the cooperation of others......

Thank you.

# Barely Live: An extended introduction to *Piece For A Pending Performance* <sub>2015</sub>
## Cally Spooner

In *Piece For A Pending Performance*, a traveling salesman, played by an actor, walks into shot (static camera), looks around, opens up his traveling case, and removes his own stage. He punches the air, then whips around to face his camera. "Hello!" (*excessive smile*) "I'm Tom!" For the next eighteen (increasingly unhinged) minutes, it becomes clear that Tom has nothing to sell, but his own delivery, and nothing in his briefcase except his thin black stage.

Tom Stuart, an actor, performed this role—which we developed together over three uproarious rehearsals and a live performance at Camden Arts Centre. The following year, when I'd receive invitations to perform (exhibition openings, performance events, etc.), I would send Tom in my place. Charging unannounced into venues, he would channel his inner deranged door-to-door salesman, shaking out his stage like a tourist with a beach towel. Sweating, shouting, he'd perform the script then leave the building, scooping up his briefcase and retrieving his jacket—shed fifteen minutes prior in a fit of elation: "I am who I am, and who I am... [throws jacket] ...is public."

This script is very personal. When I started making work it was always live and I would perform it myself. I was trying to come as close as possible to live, nascent communication (using speech, anxieties, actual conversations, and last-minute changes of mind as my unrehearsed material). I considered these forces to be more vital—more poetic and political—than fixed objects.

The performances would take weeks to create then disappear in minutes, procuring just speech and dog-eared, pen-scrawled scripts (which I'd lose or throw out). Once my performances arrived, I believed they should never arrive again. I was using them to work out new potentials and there was no sense in working out something twice. *Piece For A Pending Performance* comes out of my desire to keep making such work, while knowing that this work was exhausting me; my immaterial workload was becoming insane.

Equally, the script is a response to Paulo Virno's thesis, *Grammar of the Multitude* (2001), which I came upon quite late (in 2010). I was glad to have had some years oblivious to it—his damning critique of immaterial labor totally messed up my fandom for speech and vitalism. Convincingly laying out how capital reproduces itself through communication and continually invests in the power of living matter and speech (controlling the social codes of all that lives), Virno forced me to rethink things.

This monologue script is a slapstick translation of Virno's text. I wrote it to understand his thesis better, because I also felt decimated by this same post-Fordist condition; endlessly producing immaterially, urgently, on demand. How does a laboring body (that leaves no external work behind) step away from its work? To be consistently laboring—a biological flow—is an inescapable human condition, and a laborless life would be a strange kind of delegated existence, but when there is no externalization—no product—where does the labor go? It might stick in the throat, in the body, and then what does this do to your voice, metabolism, disclosure, politics, instincts, relationships? Do these become instrumental to your high performance? Do they become *only* labor? Are they tools with which to compete? How do you rest? Where do you go? When is your speech *not* at work? These questions really floored me.

Filming *Piece For A Pending Performance* was, unsurprisingly, hectic. Tom, who is brilliantly disorganized, always had to be somewhere else too early, usually at an audition. On shoot day, it was a fiftieth birthday party at 3 p.m. We couldn't work the boom mic, so shooting delayed to 2:40 p.m., and at 3:05, as Tom ran out of shot and into a waiting taxi, I had no footage other than our first and only straight take (and no money to rebook the camera or Tom). So *Piece For A Pending Performance* became an unedited, first, straight take to camera with pretty shoddy sound. I'm hugely attached to the film (even more than any of my live work) on the basis that it very nearly doesn't exist at all. Even the sound, for me, is perfect.

I always think living work could be defined by being largely undesigned; allowed to land where it lands, in the margins of last-minuteness. This means that most work that promises to be live just isn't (like Britney's *Piece Of Me* residency in Las Vegas or *Cats the Musical*—thirty-four years running). On the other hand, a lot of things that are definitely not considered live can be more alive than anything that is (in theory) living. But I only learned this recently, by making more single-take and first-take films with casts and crews.

When I think about how capital has become a semiotic operator, and the kinds of communication it is producing—such as managerial discourse—I realize how mechanized and overly rehearsed these techniques are. They resemble the worst, most over-worked play; the semiotic equivalent of Britney, who has performed her greatest show on earth live over two hundred times without deviation: "What's up!!? How you guys feeling!? Cheers. It's so awesome to be with you here tonight. Isn't this theater beautiful?"

If I stop in WHSmiths at London Waterloo station (which isn't a very big WHSmiths), I can pick up twenty books that teach me about these semiotics in less than two hundred pages. The back blurb is phrased around openness; how to create and lead the spaces for new stuff to happen, in oneself and in others. And, yes, that sounds like my own live work ideologies. Right now, I am really trying to find the difference between those books and my work.

Unless I'm talking about a can opener, I absolutely hate the word "effective." The fact of the matter is that while they might not look like it, these "open techniques" are industrially designed to be effective. I guess the main difference then between my work and the books is that the techniques of the latter are designed to leave all the space for chance operations and liveliness in terms of content, while leaving nothing to chance when it comes to *promises* to be *effective* in reproducing capitalism. They have been trialed and tested. The books probably have a money-back guarantee. In *The Open Work*, Umberto Eco talks about how the trait of industrial design is that it is never irksome. It's always a well-oiled cliché. Even if it's pretending to be opaque, it's absolutely solid.

These semiotic techniques borrow (probably unwittingly) from forms of openness that we see in cultural productions, which have committed to working with forms of life and living matter. I am thinking of the New York School's improvisatory scores (such as Earle Brown's December 1952 "structure," which enables performers to, essentially, innovate). Or even the methods that Mike Leigh uses (and that I also often use in directing) to *devise* films rather than design and plan them out in advance. (Leigh famously refuses to provide a script or shot list, leaving space for the genius and bright ideas of his cast.)

When I watch Leigh's films or see/hear a score by Brown, I absolutely trust that the desires that drive their outputs are fundamental to the drive to be with and listen to other people. While Brown, as an author, of course, desired to make a masterful score and hoped to see impressive, well-rounded performances of it, he was not exactly aiming at an effective musical monument for personal growth or gain: "I wanted to make a field of activity, of music, a making activity... for sympathetic and reasonable kinds of people."[1]

As much as is possible, I want my work to trust in time and people. It is so much better to come upon and be convivial with new people than to not. It is possible to find and create social knowledge in these negotiations. Sure, there is a big drive underneath this, which is my own authorship, and, yes, I also know that there are contradictions riddled throughout this text—whether I am able to produce a politically processed subject (me, others, audiences? I don't know…) or whether, through my heavy usage of live bodies and real time, I am also consuming and commodifying that which lives for my own authorship. However, for now, right now today, I do know that my primary desire is *not to generate capital for myself or for shareholders*.

Today, my desire is to generate well-researched, time-rich writing that can be used as scripts or devising structures. Within these, unlikely alliances of people, time frames, contexts, and convivial forces can assemble, rupture existing understanding of how something should arrive or be made, and then disassemble. I wish to try and find a completely new model for making work with other people, one that upsets previous models I have used and does not rely on the limitations of humanist foundations that I often default to as justification for making work "responsibly" and "creatively" with living bodies. I know this language and these foundations are inadequate.

I wish to create a sustainable, modern way of working that is not opposed to the dominant hierarchies it is trying to differ itself from, and does not evade the fact of power relations (both positive and restrictive) that inevitably envelop it. Instead, it attempts to speak with knowledge of these and through these. I wish to work with consideration and awareness of the sites I am dependent on (institutions) and to not forget that these are a primary material in my work, because they have the power to employ me.

I am interested in how the responsibility I think I have, as a producer who works with performers, can migrate into a more leaderless condition—less ownership for me—while being quite afraid of this possibility. And I wish to find ways of working with others that are suitable and appropriate to the people that happen to come together for temporary periods of time, and how that time can be (borrowing from Brecht) fun—fun that arrives only through a *protracted period of seriousness*. I wish for the methods that we use to work together to be created in response to the group that forms. This is not primarily nor deliberately for the sake of fresh, new technologies of management, nor for endlessly innovating my work, but simply because it's way more interesting and affirming for everyone involved.

I choose to research, network, and apply for funding, and from this, I wish to pay myself and others to work, so that we can be clearly remunerated (because we all need to eat, pay rent/mortgages, and take care of any dependents, and working while becoming decimated by financial exhaustion is the opposite of life-affirming). I wish for appropriate crediting for the work that is created, work that should, eventually, evolve into something external and nameable, and that can be understood and critiqued by those who were involved in its arrival. And while I am not doing all of this all the time, today, this is what I understand to be live work.

For now… For me, *Piece For A Pending Performance* is fragile. And marvelous: because of Tom, because the boom broke, because it was personal, because we were really *trying* to see what could happen, because it's the first "external product" that exists away from my body (and away from Tom's body), because it's a process that I couldn't entirely control, and that could only have been exactly what it was and is. On this basis, *Piece For A Pending Performance* is very much a living gesture.

Notes

1 Earle Brown, *December 1952*, 1970. Monologue recording. Earle Brown Music Foundation, <http://www.earle-brown.org/archive.focus.php?id=726>.

Cally Spooner

# I want to talk again about the birds who are deaf from fireworks <sub>2015</sub>

## Jason Dodge

Here is a list of the things we will remember:
bird lights, vapor lights, mud lights, neon
lights, and city lights selling and taking, selling and taking away.

These women are in a higher state; everything told to them is told by wind and leaves
and trash blowing all around in there. Birds
deaf from fireworks blowing around in there.

I found in my neighbor's trash an empty
bottle of lice treatment and hair dye, and I
wonder who sleeps with her, and I hope that
someone sleeps with her.

In my neighborhood, everyone is a young
mother with tattoos pushing baby strollers,
drinking something from a takeaway cup.
Take away, take it all away.

+

I understand the fight or flight instinct; it is
the teetering between states of consciousness.
It is the vibrations that are chemicals tripping
one pin or another pin. It is the tiny gondola
on my pen from Venice, sliding back and forth
in some mysterious liquid.

I want to talk again about the birds<br>
who are deaf from fireworks

These days, I am thinking about the hexag-
onal storm on the north pole of Saturn; it
could consume seven Earths. We could not
see it in the winter because it was too dark,
and because the winter on Saturn began
eighty years ago and before the darkness,
we didn't have lenses that could look at the
storm. Now it is spring, and there is light
on the hurricane again and there will be for
eighty years before the dankness comes.

I understand the fight or flight instinct, but I
do not understand the way people scatter at
the café when the wasps come, humiliating
themselves, setting up cups of sugar water, and
waving the air around and ducking. Believe
the wasps, they are tiny sapphires and aqua-
marines, garnets and jades—let them drink
your wine, let them taste your cake; their days
are numbered, the season is coming to an end.

I understand the fight or flight instinct, but
I do not understand the "kill it" part when
visited by wasps.

Remember, you should invent a name before
you tear off its wings, and you have to swallow

the wings and crush the body under your glass, because moments before it became your death machine, it was filled with tea picked in Africa and touching your lips.

Dear stranger, I love the way you are sitting there with your legs crossed taking pictures, waving your telephone around like a mirror collecting all of the light it has reflected, reflecting everything to keep it. And you sing, "Refract tiny moth, live here in my transmitting device, we will spin silk from our lenses together and post it online so that everyone knows there is a new oration that is posted online."

+

How did you choose your PIN code. Is it initials? A date? Was it chosen for you by your bank? Is it the birthday of your true love or the day they were born?

Every time you enter your PIN code, you launch ships from harbors in Korea in the middle of the night and India in the middle of the afternoon. Plastic parts, interlocking parts, spring-loaded parts, and glass, tempered and untempered, loaded by people wearing masks and rubber gloves, putting things in bags, putting bags in boxes, putting boxes into containers, loading containers onto ships.

Your new refrigerator is waiting two years from now—all the tiny parts will keep your yoghurt cold, your milk, the food from the night before, all the delicious things you thought about eating—you hold the spoon and place it in your love's mouth while only looking at their eyes.

Next time you type your PIN code into the PIN code terminal, think of the other finger-tips that have been there just before, try to flip it in your mind, make it a tiny pool of water, and think of the last fingers coming up to the surface, making tiny rings of water that vibrate out as they touch your fingers.

Now, think about how they are also walking around, lungs moving back and forth, carry-ing thoughts around in their bodies. All that thump, thump of our hearts beating together somehow; everything with a heart shimmer-ing together, some beating for the first time and others the last.

Jason Dodge

+

Meanwhile, your eyes are looking at my eyes on the screen and not the camera on the top of the screen, so it looks like you are looking at my nose.

It is that ancient measure again—the ten centimeters that expands to be precisely the distance between us; the ten centimeters between the camera on your computer and my eyes.

It is the measure that keeps our eyes from meeting. We know about this, about this space, this bend calculation, because it was the dream of the Sumerians to find a way to speak with anyone when they are not near, when they are far away, out of sight. Now, we are the new letters and messengers.

On the computer, when we were speaking, you were smoking. The white on the end of your cigarette would pulse and get bigger. You were sitting in the dark so the white ember of your cigarette was pulsing and then waving around making streaks and then coming to your mouth again and glowing, and you inhaled a bright white spot and exhaled blur, and then a smaller moving white spot. Etc.

When we were speaking on the computer, I noticed that as you were smoking, the yellow on the end of your cigarette pulsed and got bigger. You were sitting in the dark so the yellow and green were pulsing, and then waving around making streaks and then coming to your mouth and glowing again as you inhaled smoke so that I couldn't see it, and then a green spot and then a smaller moving color. Etc.

The other day, someone was telling me about synesthesia—a neurological condition in which the mind ascribes a color to every word. Multiplying, in colors, I am trying to imagine what it feels like in the brain; what color a word like "retroactively" is. She was telling me this story because she was talking about her daughter who is a polyglot and seems to be able to remember languages after hearing them the first time. She was telling her daughter about synesthesia—she was thirteen and could speak seven or eight languages—and her daughter said, "You don't see colors?"

When we were speaking through the computer, I noticed that as you were the orange on the end of your cigarette, you would pulse in the dark. The orange ember of your cigarette was pulsing and then waving around making streaks and then to your mouth and then glowing again; an orange spot and then a smaller moving red spot. Etc.

On a flight, I woke up and on the screens hanging from the ceiling was a program of people falling. People falling who didn't want to fall, or who didn't expect to fall. The film with people falling was funny, I could tell by the editing; the same scene over and over, sometimes just the moment of falling, sometimes it was slow motion, sometimes it was very slow motion of just the moment of impact, and the Coca-Cola splashing.

An enormous woman and an ice cream were falling. After she finished falling, the ice cream fell on her. She was falling, and on her face and in her eyes was the expression of falling—after she had fallen, the ice cream was still falling and then it wasn't falling.

I want to talk again about the birds<br>who are deaf from fireworks

Someone made this film with his or her telephone. They made the film with their telephone and then sent it to the TV station so that everyone could watch it in super slow motion, over and over, while they were not falling, but being propelled by jet engines burning massive amounts of fuel—an unimaginable amount of fuel that came from under oceans—then a child fell, and the old man fell, and the skater fell in one direction and his skateboard flew in another, a cat fell in one direction and a glass of water rolled over and the water fell, the water fell on the child whose reaction scared the cat, and I imagined myself there on the row of screens, saying over and over in my head, I am going to fall, I am falling, I have fallen—but we were not falling, we were landing.

What are we saying when we tell ourselves,
"It will be alright,"
"Will it be all right?," "Will this be ok?" over and over?

I have landed in England.

I am in England.

Jason Dodge

How do I leave England?

+

There are things that are not individual—like
flocks of birds and forests of trees and trees
of leaves and meadows of grass, which can
become bales, and money exchangeable for
anything of its value. I am looking for a way
to talk about coins, how we all have the same
faces in our pockets on tiny metal disks and
that the heat from our bodies transfers for a
short time to these tiny pieces of metal while
we hand them off for some small exchanges. I
was watching our dog smelling coins that had
fallen on the floor, watching her brain retrace
all of the tiny transactions, all the paths that
those coins have taken, all the hands, all the
warm hands. Let's stop yelling at her when
she is barking, she thinks it is a chorus.

I love talking about rain because I like the part
about how in a raindrop, there is Napoleon's
sweat and the pee of thousands of dogs and
the blood of insects, and that for a crystal
of snow to form, there must be a particle
of something; what lands on your tongue is
a crystal that has formed around a speck of

I want to talk again about the birds
who are deaf from fireworks

pollen, ash from a volcano, a fleck of skin. I am curious about what is ancient as opposed to what is not.

How do I know or not know if that is the same bee that I noticed yesterday? When I say, "That bird," do I mean every bird that looks like that? Any coin is exchangeable for anything of its value—metal disks with tiny faces; they hold the heat from your hand for a moment before being passed off to another hand.

I love talking about rain because I like the part about how a raindrop has Napoleon's sweat and the pee of thousands of dogs in it, and that for a crystal of snow to form there has to be a particle of something; what covers the top of that car are snowflakes that formed around a grain of pollen, dust, a fleck of skin.

The tree out there is blooming again. Someday, it will be firewood or a chair, there are many uses.

There's the V of geese again; they leave, they come back, they leave.

I am trying to figure out if the bumblebees
swarming around that pile of shit is some
kind of warning.

Do you know different names for wind?

How many different metals can you think
of? Do you feel more connected to one than
another?

Are there fish that glow in the dark?

What time of day do you like the least?

What is a cloudburst?

Can we blame animals?

When you don't know who is calling, what
does your voice sound like when you answer
the phone?

How old were you when you realized that
you were surrounded by electricity?

Do you think actual information is exchanged
between plants and birds?

I want to talk again about the birds<br>
who are deaf from fireworks

Between birds and ash?

Birds and ash and coins?

Hello air full of pollen.

Hello half bottle of water.

Is it the news online that is supposed to catch my attention?

Or is it the meaning of the tiger's cage?

I don't think that was a flowerpot falling off of someone's balcony, I think it was someone closing a car door that you heard.

I have spent the last hour breaking boxes down for recycling. Kicking the sides out, pushing them into themselves. Holding them down while I tie them into bundles, and then I push the bundles into the blue bin instead of the orange bin—trying to make them fit, pressing them all together, trying to make the lid still close.

Jason Dodge

All of the pets got out. It was not a revolt or out of disgust, it was just a compulsion for beast to join beast, for cats to make their prides, and dogs their packs roaming the streets learning to kill for food again. The yellow birds and red birds, brown and white, blue and pink in a flock, dense like mud and blocking out the sunlight, learning to find berries and seeds again, and to kill for food again, flies and gnats, sometimes even smaller birds. "This is progress," they said.

I want to talk again about the birds
who are deaf from fireworks

# Be Still and Still Moving <sup></sup>2016

## Courtenay Finn

In the winter of 1983, artist David Hammons stood in New York's Cooper Square selling snowballs. Arranged in neat rows on a piece of colorful fabric, the snowballs in Hammons's *Bliz-aard Ball Sale* (1983) blended in with the other wares and trinkets being sold on the street corner. Cited as one of the best examples of the artist's elusive, often ephemeral practice, Hammons's act of selling snow in the dead of winter treads the fine line between magic and trickery—a position that he continues, time and time again, to take. Depending on how we approach the work, Hammons is either pulling a fast one on us, or alternatively, peddling time itself. Each snowball is an object of time. And in selling time, Hammons not only evokes the very "liveness" that exists within contemporary art, but also within life itself.

In a similar context, artist Allan Kaprow's practice embodies the blurred space between art and life, positing questions around the notion of presence, the body, and what constitutes "liveness." He wrote, "If a flexible framework with the barest limits is established by selecting, for example, only five elements out of an infinity of possibilities, almost anything can happen."[1] By setting up a structure for exchange without defining how the encounter should look or feel, or what it should result in, Kaprow created a scenario in which "something spontaneous, something that just happens to happen" occurs. As a result, he produced a series of impromptu and unscripted environments, activities, and Happenings—situations where the line between art and life was kept purposely fluid.

Hammons's *Bliz-aard Ball Sale* equally acknowledges that actions produce effects. And like Kaprow, rather than focusing on the effect itself, his interest lies in the very fact that the effect exists. Both artists are concerned less with the measure of achievement and instead emphasize how a live structure can generate active possibility. Exemplifying the unpredictable and performative nature of "liveness," both Kaprow and Hammons created scenarios that reveled in the wonder of the unexpected and unknown. Their works remind us that we lead fragile, but marvelous lives—fragile in the sense that we have no control over what happens and marvelous for the very same reason.

The title of this exhibition, *A Fragile But Marvelous Life*, is taken from a quote by Kaprow: "Our advanced art approaches a fragile but marvelous life, one that maintains itself by a mere thread, melting into an elusive, changeable configuration, the surroundings, the artist, his work and everyone who comes to it."[2] Directly inspired by both Kaprow and Hammons, the show operates as a live structure, presenting a series of works that ask us to be still, but still moving. Upon entering the gallery, the audience is thrust into a scenario where objects move at their own speed and where the fluidity of time is ever-present. The works create a bewildering, but marvelous feeling of entering into something already in motion—an experience that artist Sharon Hayes has spoken about directly. "When you come into the middle of something, like a bike race for instance or a choreographed dance, whether you're a rider or a dancer or you've just come to watch, you have to jump in at that point and go forward or otherwise you can't keep up."[3] Hayes continues, "You don't even think to ask 'How long have they been dancing?' 'Have there always been eight of them?' 'When did they start moving in unison?' Instead you accept what is there as if it was always there."[4]

Developed out of her live musical *And You Were Wonderful, On Stage* (2013), Cally Spooner's performance piece *Tough Kid, Full Out. True Pro. Get Better, Rest Up, Strange Night but... Proud* (2014–15) is a chorus line of voices that appears unannounced in the exhibition space. With a melody that begins comfortably reminiscent of pop music, *Tough Kid* interjects itself into the gallery, taking center stage. Yet, as it gets progressively faster and louder, it becomes clear that the work has its own agenda, although what that is remains unclear. *Tough Kid* explores the transformation of emotion into a professional strategy, addressing the very state of human communication where, more often than not, emphasis is placed singularly on results rather than the discourse itself. Though Spooner's singers are performing live within the exhibition space, the "liveness" within the work results through language and spoken word's ability to affect bodies in space.

Emily Roysdon's *Uncounted* (2014) is a free takeaway poster stacked on a blue powder-coated aluminum wave. Presented as a gift to the exhibition's audience, the poster stack slowly shrinks over time, juxtaposing the movement of bodies with the rhythm of language. A subtle and simple gesture, *Uncounted* posits Roysdon's query, "How to be alive in a museum?" Putting forth a possible answer, she goes on to say, "Make nothing happen… and revel in the uncounted." The gesture of making nothing happen reveals time's malleable form, highlighting the inherent "liveness" in simply being present.

While Roysdon takes the position of staying put, arguing for the need to take one's time, Spooner uses the presence of other bodies to redirect and refocus our attention back onto ourselves. Both works ask us to take stock of who, what, and where we are. Roysdon's slowly disappearing paper stack and Spooner's musical interruption embody different modes of "liveness," with the pairing of fast and slow revealing the passing of time itself.

In 1968, artist Ian Wilson decided to make his final sculpture, preferring instead to work within the framework of spoken language—where the speech act becomes a mode of creation. Wilson's piece *Time (Spoken)* (1982) makes its presence known whenever visitors inquire about the work, asking the invariable question: "Where or what is Ian Wilson's piece *Time (Spoken)*?" What they hear in return is an echo of their own question—the work is the word "time" being spoken out loud. Occupying a temporal space, Wilson's piece lives on outside the exhibition—the very essence of the work being the possibility that it can be realized by anyone anywhere at anytime.

In artist Roman Ondák's *Clockwork* (2014), a museum attendant stands in an empty gallery. Throughout the duration of the exhibition, whenever anyone walks into the room, the attendant asks two questions: "What time is it?" and "What is your name?" The attendant then records visitors' responses on the gallery wall. *Clockwork* begins as an empty white room, but slowly becomes a shared terrain of action. Time begins to have its own presence, becoming a quality as much as a chronology.

Operating in between visibility and invisibility, both Wilson and Ondák reveal the fluidity of form. When shown together, the connection between *Clockwork* and *Time (Spoken)* becomes live. One work activates the other, creating a space in which time and its passing are wholly evident.

In 1965, artist Robert Breer began to work on a series of kinetic sculptures that he referred to as "floats." His "motorized mollusks," as the artist also described them, are simple forms that float through space at a speed almost imperceptible to the eye—their movement only disrupted when they encounter an obstacle. Creating objects that embody cinematic movement, Breer set out to show how human interaction or intervention can be a form of animation. "When did the floats appear? How did they get to be Styrofoam and move around? I was looking for material that's lightweight that I could manipulate. So there it was. I didn't like it because it was so damn fragile. But then I did like it because it was fragile. Because if it was fragile it was an expression of the ephemeralness."[5] Breer's description reveals his interest in objects that embody time, their material essence personifying the temporality of the live. Moving through the exhibition at their own speed, the floats constantly change the configuration and orientation of the space, creating an endless loop—a space without beginning or end.

Roelof Louw's *Soul City (Pyramid of Oranges)* (1967) consists of 5,800 oranges arranged into the shape of a pyramid. Visitors are invited to take an orange as they pass through the exhibition, and as a result, the pyramid's shape continues to change until it eventually disappears. A decomposing multiple, whose physical body is consumed by the audience, *Soul City* exemplifies Louw's interest in creating sculptures that, rather than simply being looked at, are meant to be experienced, challenging the definition of sculpture as a fixed, static object. Yet, it is his use of the orange, with its recognizable smell, shape, and color, that reminds us how material has the uncanny ability to convey thought, feeling, time, and memory.

Both Breer's floats and Louw's oranges occupy different modes of time. In Louw's case, it is evident within the material itself—the orange's lifespan is entirely dependent on time, temperature, and touch. For Breer, it occurs in the vulnerability of the space that the floats occupy, their movements unrestricted and uncontrolled. Though the floats' movements are slow and methodical, they have an intrinsic fragility that is entirely independent from the temporal landscape we ourselves inhabit.

Artist, filmmaker, and choreographer Yvonne Rainer once wrote to fellow artist and friend Sturtevant, "Don't despair. Keep working. You know the dance."[6] The line, "You know the dance," evokes a kinaesthetic awareness—the understanding that one's body knows where it is in time and space, and can and will change its configuration accordingly. Our bodies hold within them automated movements, executed without thought. There is comfort within this muscle memory, within the physical movements by which we move and perform in the world. Yet, it is in situations that jolt us out of this automation that we can begin to see and feel our world anew.

Mika Rottenberg's *Ponytails* (2014) consists of three disembodied ponytails coming through the gallery wall. Removed from any perceivable head or body, they bounce, jump, and flip with the implied action of a human body. By isolating just the ponytail, Rottenberg asks us to reexamine our relationship to everyday movement as well as to hair itself. How we wear and style our hair is a facet of how we present ourselves to the world, a transaction that blurs the boundary between personal desire and public reception. Removed from the human body, the ponytail becomes a byproduct and symbol for the way in which we see, recognize, judge, or dismiss one another in the world. Rottenberg's ponytails reframe the relationship between bodies and objects, creating "liveness" through the activation of a seemingly ordinary item.

Sergei Tcherepnin's *Motor-Matter Bench* (2013) is a New York City subway bench outfitted with surface transducers—devices that convert signals into vibrations, allowing anything to become a speaker. Visitors are invited to sit and experience Tcherepnin's composition as felt through physical vibrations. By playing the sound through people sitting on the bench, Tcherepnin not only creates intimacy between audience and object, but listening also becomes a physical act. The artist reframes the everyday experience of sitting and waiting for the train to arrive, turning an ordinary act into something extraordinary.

Both Rottenberg's ponytails and Tcherepnin's bench examine the relationship between how we perform as people in the world and how we perform within the context of the museum. By inviting us to reexamine our understanding of performativity, Rottenberg and Tcherepnin make us aware of our action and time in space, providing a complex meditation on time, existence, and our relationship to art and life.

Courtenay Finn

Time is the protagonist, the central character around which everything in the exhibition revolves. Yet, it is not simply the linear time of the clock or calendar, but also the space we devote to our own experience—the "content" dimension of time, as writer John Berger aptly termed it.[7] The works in *A Fragile But Marvelous Life*, both individually and collectively, serve to remind us that time is measured by living. They use time as a pliable form to create a framework that encourages slowing down and being present, evoking the "liveness" inherent in Hammons's snowballs or in Kaprow's Happenings—still and still moving.

Recently, I reread a book from my childhood, Michael Ende's *Momo*, which centers on a series of gray gentlemen who feed on time. Representing a large time-saving bank, the men convince the adults of the world to deposit their time, earning valuable interest in the form of more time. The more people save, the less time they have. By giving up any time not seen as productive—such as that allotted for play, leisure, and pleasure—the world becomes sterile, lifeless, and gray. Faced with this grayness, everyone works harder, trying to save more time, not noticing that their actions are causing the gray gentlemen to gain strength. It is left to a small child named Momo, blessed with the gift of listening, to fix the situation. Setting out to stop the gentlemen from stealing everyone's time, Momo shows us, "Time is life itself, and life resides in the human heart."[8]

While reading *Momo*, I remembered an interview with artist Kris Martin in which he talks about the relationship between time and life: "We try to understand time and capture it, but it is simply not possible. As a consequence, time is so interesting and beautiful. Everything that we can control becomes uninteresting; the things we cannot control are still the most beautiful ones. You cannot control the sunset, but everyone likes it. With time, it is the same. Everything is time, and we are just part of it."[9]

Everything is time, and we are just part of it.

Notes

1    Allan Kaprow, "Happenings in the New York Scene (1961)," in *Essays on the Blurring of Art and Life*, ed. Jeff Kelley (Berkeley: University of California Press, 2003), 20.

2    Ibid., 18.

3    Sharon Hayes, "Keynote Lecture: The Creative Time Summit: Revolutions in Public Practice," in *Coming After: Queer Time, Arriving Too Late and the Spectre of the Recent Past* (Toronto: The Power Plant, 2012), 61.

4    Ibid.

5    Paul Cummings, *Oral History Interview with Robert Breer*, July 10, 1973 <http://www.aaa.si.edu/collections/interviews/oral-history-interview-robert-breer-11951> (accessed October 1, 2015).

6    Bruce Hainley, "First Position: The Early Performance Work of Sturtevant," *Artforum* Vol. 50, Issue 7 (March 2012).

7    John Berger, *And Our Faces, My Heart, Brief as Photos* (New York: Vintage International, 1991), 35.

8    Michael Ende, *Momo* (London: Penguin Books, 1984), 60.

9    Karlyn De Jongh, "I Want Your Imagination: A Conversation with Kris Martin," *Sculpture* Vol. 28, No. 8 (October 2009), 29.

Courtenay Finn

# Director's Afterword
## Heidi Zuckerman

This publication is both the companion catalogue to the exhibition *A Fragile But Marvelous Life*, presented at the Aspen Art Museum from November 20, 2015–February 7, 2016, and a collection of writing around the role of "liveness" within contemporary culture.

First, I want to thank Courtenay Finn, AAM Curator, who addressed the relationship between everyday movement and performance in a subtle, intelligent, and thoughtful way, curating an exhibition that reminds us of the value of looking closely.

I am honored to include in this publication a series of texts by an incredible group of artists. Throughout the pieces, some published here for the first time, Robert Breer, Jason Dodge, Courtenay Finn, Allan Kaprow, William Pope.L, Emily Roysdon, and Cally Spooner address "liveness" as a generative force, breaking apart traditional modes of representation and opening up different modes of engagement. I am grateful for their thoughtful and illuminating contributions, all of which have made this a richer publication.

*A Fragile But Marvelous Life* is funded in part by the Aspen Art Museum National Council. One hundred percent of its contributions support the museum's exhibitions, financial assistance for which we are ever grateful. General support for this exhibition is provided by the Diane and Bruce Halle Foundation for Latin American Art, the Toby Devan Lewis Visiting Artist Fund, and the Marx Exhibition Fund. The museum's profound gratitude goes to Toby Devan Lewis who has permanently endowed the AAM's Publications Fund.

My sincere thanks go to the Board of Trustees and the entire staff of the Aspen Art Museum—this exhibition and publication would not have been possible without the cooperation, determination, and enthusiasm of each and every one involved. The exhibition was overseen by Director of Exhibitions and Registration, Luis Yllanes, and Installation Director, Jonathan Hagman, with assistance from Curatorial Associate and Archivist, Sherry Black, and Associate Registrar, Elen Woods. The catalogue was beautifully conceived and developed by designer, Sara Fowler, and edited by AAM Editor, Sarah Stephenson.

I am grateful to the following institutions and individuals for making loans from their collections possible: Andrea Rosen Gallery, New York; Collection Antoine de Galbert, Paris; Collection Chaussinand et Lebrun, Paris; Kate Flax; Heather Flow; Flow Advisory; gb agency, Paris; Jan Mot, Brussels; Richard Saltoun Gallery, London; and Tate, London.

Finally, I would like to thank the artists included in *A Fragile But Marvelous Life*—Robert Breer, Roelof Louw, Roman Ondák, Mika Rottenberg, Emily Roysdon, Cally Spooner, Sergei Tcherepnin, and Ian Wilson—as it is their insightful and engaging work that allows us to see the world anew.

Heidi Zuckerman
Nancy and Bob Magoon CEO and Director

# Contributors

Robert Breer was an experimental filmmaker, painter, and sculptor. Over his extensive and acclaimed fifty-year career, highlights include: a retrospective at the Whitney Museum, New York (1980); a solo show at Staff USA/AC Project Room, New York (1999); a film retrospective at the Centre Georges Pompidou, Paris, in combination with a solo exhibition at gb agency, Paris (2001). More recently, his films have been exhibited in *Le Mouvement des Images* at the Museé national d'art moderne, Paris (2006). His sculptures were shown at Kunsthalle Basel (2007); the Secession, Vienna (2009); and a solo show in CAPC, Bordeaux (2010). A retrospective touring show was presented at Baltic Centre for Contemporary Art, Gateshead, and Museum Tinguely, Basel (2011). His film *Fuji* was registered in the permanent film collection of the Library of Congress, Washington, DC, in 2002. In 2005, Breer received the prestigious Stan Brakhage Vision Award in Denver, Colorado.

Jason Dodge is an artist living in Berlin.

Courtenay Finn is the Curator at the Aspen Art Museum, Colorado. Recent exhibitions curated by Finn at the AAM include Anna Sew Hoy's *Magnetic Between, The Blue of Distance, Stories We Tell Ourselves*, and Alice Channer's *R o c k f a l l*. From 2011–14, she was the Curator at Art in General, New York, where she curated Art in General's first international new commission with Lebanese artist Mounira Al Solh. In 2013, she was the co-curator of

*North by Northeast*, the Latvian Pavilion's presentation for the 55th edition of the Venice Biennale. Finn received her MA in Curatorial Practice at the California College for the Arts, San Francisco, in 2008, and her BFA from the Cleveland Institute of Art, Ohio, in 2005.

Allan Kaprow was an American painter, assemblagist, and a pioneer in establishing the concepts of performance art. Kaprow's first Happening, *Eighteen Happenings in Six Parts*, took place in October 1959 at Reuben Gallery in New York. Major solo exhibitions of Kaprow's work have taken place recently at Tate Modern, London; Geffen Contemporary at the Museum of Contemporary Art, Los Angeles (both 2008); Van Abbemuseum, Eindhoven, the Netherlands; Kunsthalle Bern, Switzerland; Museo di Arte Contemporanea di Villa Groce, Genoa, Italy (all 2007); and Haus der Kunst, Munich (2006). Kaprow was awarded National Endowment for the Arts awards in 1974 and 1979, and a John Simon Guggenheim fellowship in 1979.

Charles Levine was a filmmaker who lived and worked in New York.

Matt Olson works on projects related to contemporary art and design: landscape and environments, furniture and objects, actions and scenarios, teaching and writing. On 01/01/16, he began OOIEE (the Office of Int.\Est.\Ext. [Interior Establishes Exterior]) as a new backdrop for exploring the intersections of time and perception as they relate to space and the objects that fill it. Olson embraces an "open practice" in the belief that following forward and trusting the work presented by the world becomes a poetic collaboration with the great "everything." He was formerly the Cofounder/Creative Director of RO/LU, whose work has been shown internationally and resides in the permanent collection of the Walker Art Center as well as many esteemed private collections. He currently teaches "Towards A Cross Disciplinary Open Practice" in the School of Architecture at the University of Minnesota. He was featured in the *PIN-UP Interviews* compendium and his first book, *What Would Anything be Without Everything Else*, will be published by Powerhouse in 2016. OOIEE's first action took place at the Aspen Art Museum in February 2016 followed by an exhibit of new furniture pieces in May through Patrick Parrish Gallery in New York.

William Pope.L is a Chicago-based interdisciplinary artist best known for his performance work and his decades-long series of crawls, commemorated in *eRacism*, a retrospective that traveled to several prominent museums and galleries across the United States between 2002 and 2004. Recent solo exhibitions and performances include *Trinket*, the Geffen Contemporary, Museum of Contemporary Art, Los Angeles; *Cage Unrequited*, MCA Live, Museum of Contemporary Art, Chicago (both 2015); *Media Replication Services*, Whitney Museum of American

Art, New York; *Gold People Shit In Their Valet*, Galerie Catherine Bastide, Brussels (both 2014); *Colored Waiting Room*, Mitchell-Innes & Nash, New York; *Foreslen*, the Renaissance Society, University of Chicago; and *Pull*, SPACES, Cleveland, Ohio (all 2013). Pope.L is the recipient of many prestigious grants and awards, including the Guggenheim Fellowship, NEA fellowships, Tiffany Foundation Award, Nancy Graves Foundation Award, and the United States Artists Rockefeller Fellowship.

Emily Roysdon is a New York– and Stockholm-based artist and writer. Roysdon completed the Whitney Museum Independent Study Program in 2001 and an Interdisciplinary MFA at UCLA in 2006. She is editor and cofounder of the queer feminist journal and artist collective LTTR. Her many collaborations include costume design for choreographers Levi Gonzalez, Vanessa Anspaugh, and Faye Driscoll, as well as lyric writing for The Knife and Brooklyn-based JD Samson & MEN. Recent solo projects include new commissions from Performance Room, Tate Modern, London, PARTICIPANT, INC, New York, If I Can't Dance, Amsterdam, Portland Institute of Contemporary Art, Visual Art Center, Austin, Art in General, New York, The Kitchen, New York, Konsthall C, Stockholm, and a Matrix commission from the Berkeley Art Museum. Roysdon's work has additionally been exhibited at the Museum of Modern Art, New York, the 2010 Whitney Biennial, New York, *Greater New York* at MoMA PS1, *The*

*Generational*, New Museum, New York, Manifesta 8, Murcia and Cartagena, Spain, Museo Tamayo, Mexico City, Power Plant, Toronto, and Museo Nacional Centro de Arte Reina Sofía, Madrid.

Cally Spooner is a writer and artist living and working in London. Recent solo presentations, performances, and exhibitions include *Regardless, it's still her voice*, gb agency, Paris; *He's in a Great Place!*, BMW Live Performance Room, Tate Modern, London (both 2014); *And You Were Wonderful, On Stage*, Stedelijk Museum, Amsterdam; Performa 13, the National Academy, New York; and *Seven Thirty Till Eight*, Kunsthal Charlottenborg, Copenhagen (all 2013). 2014 projects additionally include a commission for High Line Art, New York, presentations at Frieze Film, London, and a production residency at Experimental Media and Performing Arts Centre at Rensselaer Polytechnic Institute in Troy, NY. Her novel *Collapsing In Parts* was published by Mousse in 2013, and she is a recipient of the Paul Hamlyn Foundation Awards for Artists 2013.

Executive

**Heidi Zuckerman**
Nancy and Bob Magoon
CEO and Director

**John-Paul Schaefer**
Deputy Director

**Amelia Russo**
Executive Coordinator
for the Director

Curatorial

**Sherry Black**
Curatorial Associate
and Archivist

**Courtenay Finn**
Curator

**Jonathan Hagman**
Installation Director

**Elen Woods**
Associate Registrar

**Luis Yllanes**
Director of Exhibitions
and Registration

Installation Crew and
Art Preparators
**Seth Beckton**
**Stanley Bell**
**Charles Childress**
**John Cohorst**
**Jason Cook**
**Takeo Hiromitsu**
**Ryan Jervis**
**Andrew Roberts-Gray**
**Jason Smith**

Design and Editorial

**Michael Aberman**
Design Director

**Sara Fowler**
Junior Graphic
Designer

**Sarah Stephenson**
Editor

Development

**Josh Kirrinkol**
Special Events
Assistant

**Grace Nims**
Development Director

**Melissa Prentice**
Special Events
Coordinator

**Madison Rupp**
Development
Coordinator

Education

**Michelle Dezember**
Learning Director

**Annie Henninger**
Education Program
Manager

**Morgan Lee**
Education Coordinator

Educators
**Stanley Bell**
**Jennifer Johnson**

Finance and
Administration

**Lynette Horan**
Human Resources
Manager

**Karen Johnsen**
Finance and
Administrative
Director

**Allyson Manley**
Receptionist and
Administrative
Assistant

**Holly Willson**
Accounting Clerk

Security and Visitor
Information

**Meagan Burger**
Guide Manager

**Gregg Yocom**
Senior Security Officer

Security Officers
**Manny Doron**
**Peter Feinzig**
**Bret Hitchcock**
**Jeremy Johnson**
**Siarhei Piatrovich**

Guides
Lee Azarcon
Jamie Beers
Stanley Bell
Leslie Bixel
Barrett Black
Manny Doron
Lynne Dyson
Mark Everhart
Daniel Martinez
   Granados
Rodney Hill
Bret Hitchcock
Jeremy Johnson
Lina Maldaikyte
Morgan Neely
Jess Parsons
Peiju Ritter
Ben Tomkins
Ines Vergara

Café

**Mary Daly**
Café Assistant
Manager

**Allen Domingos**
Culinary Partner

**Julia Domingos**
Culinary Partner

Café Service
Associates
**Magdalena Botello**
**Cecilia Gonzalez**
**Valerie Valenzuela**

Building and Facilities

**Kevin Haupt**
Building Engineer and
Facilities Manager

**Raimundo Martinez**
Facilities Assistant

Public Relations and
Marketing

**Katherine Peach**
Communications
Coordinator

Shop Associates
Lynne Dyson
Jennifer Johnson
Jenny Luu
Lina Maldaikyte
Peiju Ritter
Dylan Smith

This publication accompanies the exhibition *A Fragile But Marvelous Life*, curated by Courtenay Finn and on view at the Aspen Art Museum, November 20, 2015–February 7, 2016.

AAM exhibitions are made possible by the Marx Exhibition Fund. General exhibition support is provided by the Toby Devan Lewis Visiting Artist Fund.

*A Fragile But Marvelous Life* is supported by the Diane and Bruce Halle Foundation for Latin American Art, and funded in part by the AAM National Council.

Support for this publication is provided by the Toby Devan Lewis Publications Fund.

Published by
Aspen Art Press
Aspen Art Museum
637 East Hyman Avenue
Aspen, CO 81611
United States
aspenartmuseum.org



Bookmark
All photos: Tony Prikryl
Except: Ian Wilson and Sergei Tcherepnin images

Available through
ARTBOOK, LLC
Distributed Art Publishers
155 Sixth Avenue, 2nd Floor
New York, NY 10013
artbook.com

Library of Congress Cataloging-in-Publication Data
Names: Aspen Art Museum (Aspen, Colo.), organizer, host institution.
Title: A fragile but marvelous life.
Description: Aspen : Aspen Art Museum, 2016. | "This publication accompanies the exhibition A Fragile But Marvelous Life, curated by Courtenay Finn and on view at the Aspen Art Museum, November 20, 2015-February 7, 2016." | Includes bibliographical references.
Identifiers: LCCN 2016004392 | ISBN 9780934324724 (softcover)
Subjects: LCSH: Art, Modern--21st century--Themes, motives--Exhibitions. | Performative (Philosophy)--Exhibitions. | Life in art--Exhibitions.
Classification: LCC N6496.A76 A874 2016 | DDC 709.05/107478843--dc23
LC record available at http://lccn.loc.gov/2016004392

Courtenay Finn
Curator

Sherry Black
Curatorial Associate

Sarah Stephenson
Editor

Michael Aberman
Design Director

Sara Fowler
Catalogue Designer

The Avery Group at Shapco Printing Inc., Minneapolis
Printer